Spotting The Kooks

The Top 19 Kooks Who Waste Your Time, And A Venue Menu Of Great Places To Meet Your Match

Adryenn Ashley
Anjanette Harper

Published by ChickLit Media Group

Spotting The Kooks

Second Edition

Print edition ISBN: 978-0-9715679-4-8

Copyright © Chicklit Media Group 2018

All rights reserved. No part of this publication may be reproduced, stored in a retrieval system, or transmitted, in any form, or by any means, electronic, mechanical, photocopying, recording, or otherwise, without the prior consent of the publisher.

Sale of this book without a front cover may be unauthorized. If the book is coverless, it may have been reported to the publisher as "unsold or destroyed" and neither the author nor the publisher may have received payment for it.

The information presented in this book represents the views of the author as of the date of publication. This book is for informational and awareness purposes only. This book does not aim to offend any religion, caste or persons. While the situations described in the book are real, no real names have been used in order to protect the privacy of the people involved. While every attempt has been made to verify the information in this book, neither the author nor the publisher assumes any responsibility for errors, inaccuracies or omissions. Neither the publisher nor the individual author shall be liable for any physical, psychological, emotional, financial, or commercial damages, including, but not limited to, special, incidental, consequential or other damages. You are responsible for your own choices, actions, and results.

http://spottingthekooks.com

Printed in the United States of America

Table of Contents

Foreword	7
Introduction	11
The Agenda	21
The Baby	37
The Big Spender	53
The Buddy	69
The Clinger	85
The Control Freak	103
The Cyber Citizen	121
The Doom and Gloom	135
The Grifter	153
The Guru	171
The Loafer	187
The Lost	203
The Love Lover	219
The Narcissist	233
The Neatnik	251
The Solo Artist	269
The Threesome	283
The Unavailable	299
The 12-Stepper	317
The Kook In You	333

The Venue Menu 335
Online Dating 353
Certified Kook Spotter 355
About the Authors 357

Foreword

As Soulmate Coaches for spiritual, successful, single women we've heard every complaint that exists about why dating sucks and how hard it can be to find your "One." Dating can be a lot of fun or it can be a lot of heartache. It all depends on your ability to be discerning with the people you meet.

Wouldn't it be great if you had a guide that showed you how to avoid all the time/energy/money wasters you'll meet on the journey to lasting love?

Spotting The Kooks ought to be your handbook if you're tired of investing in Mr./Ms. Wrong and ending up brokenhearted... again. Adryenn and A.J. make it easy to not only identify those people you should avoid getting too attached to, they also give you the keys to getting out when you fear it's already too late.

We know from our own experience how difficult it can be to find that one person who you can truly share your life with. Reading Spotting the Kooks brought home for us how often we had dated a kook or been a kook ourselves.

This is Orna's Story:
"Never having been married until after forty I certainly had my fair share of dating kooks. The most consistent kook

for me was easy to spot as I read through the book – The Unavailable Kook! Oh how I pined for the unavailable man who would always give me just enough crumbs to not give up leaving me hoping, wishing, and praying for more.

In my twenties I encountered The Agenda Kook. He was on the track for marriage and a family. I wondered the entire time if he wanted to just get married, or if he truly wanted to marry ME. I escaped just before the ring and the question... I still wonder if he had already purchased The Ring and how narrow my escape?

The Solo Artist Kook was my first love. Clearly that did not pan out and for me it didn't end well, or pretty.

I wish that this book had been written when I was single and dating as the insights would have saved me a lot of time and agony. Being able to spot a kook (and your particular brand of kook) will illuminate the patterns you're stuck in so you can break free to have the love you want."

This is Matthew's Story:

"I may have dated a few kooks when I was younger. I will confess to being attracted to The Doom and Gloom Kook when I was in college and I spent much of my 20's chasing The Unavailable Kook. But the real value of this book is what it illuminated about my own behavior.

I was always accused of being commitment phobic by the women I dated. What I knew was that I was ambivalent about actually committing to a relationship. When I read through the book I could definitely see parts of myself in The Unavailable Kook and The Solo Artist Kook.

When I finally decided that I really wanted love; that I wanted to spend my life with one person and create a life together, all of that old behavior changed. I no longer disappeared. I stopped being The Solo Artist and started looking for my partner.

Finding Orna and creating our life together took me recognizing my old kook tendencies and doing the work to change so I could finally be available for the woman I loved.

It just goes to show that kooks can change, they just have to want to."

We know that even the best relationships can be challenging with the right person. But when that person is a certified kook then you could end up on a dead-end road to heartbreak and ruin.

Adryenn and A.J.'s tips for steering clear of the kooks not only will save you time, agony, and years in therapy – they may also give you some of the best dating advice to uplevel your dating skills so you can be discerning enough to select your Mr. or Mrs. Right.

Orna and Matthew Walters
Soulmate Coaches and founders of
Creating Love On Purpose®

Introduction

You should know right up front that I'm a reformed brazen hussy. It's part of what makes me eminently qualified to write this book! For years I sought the emotional roller coaster ride of misbegotten love affairs, jumping from boy to man to man to boy. Yeah. I got around. It's okay. I own that.

Boy could I pick 'em. (Not.) I was the girl who believed everything guys told me to get me into bed; I fell for it *every single time*. Like most children of divorce, I had a picker that was off. Big time. I desperately wanted to trust the men I fell in love with, but I was hopelessly ignorant of their lying, thieving, cheating ways.

I dated some real winners, men who were not what they seemed, men who were broken, men who were full of themselves, men who probably didn't like me much but still tried to bag me. The pinnacle of losers was the guy who told me he was the VP of a plastics company and turned out to be a drug dealer who, when I moved out, threatened to have me kidnapped, raped, and shipped to Africa to be sold into white slavery. I told you I could pick 'em.

Every relationship was fated to fail because my priorities were way out of whack. That is, until I finally wised up and got serious about finding a good match.

Tired of dating losers, I decided to go for broke and went on one hundred dates in thirty days, which basically meant I scheduled a date for breakfast, lunch, and dinner every day for an entire month. Despite the fact that I hated dating, I dove in with gusto. Working my dates like an assembly line, I got clear about my expectations. I had no choice; with so many dates, I didn't have time to mess around. And I didn't have time to fall in love blindly - be swept off my feet - or ignore warning signals that had previously slipped right past me.

After one hundreds dates I developed the ultimate picker. I could spot a catch from miles away. Better yet, I could spot the losers, jerks, and freaks I "lovingly" referred to as "kooks." Later, I parlayed my experiences as a second wife into a passion for asset protection and became a Certified Divorce Financial Analyst. And after working with scores of couples in the throes of divorce, I honed my kook detector into the fine instrument it is today.

And my co-author, AJ? Well, she earned her kook-dar the hard way, too. Spooky strangers feigning laryngitis to get a date with her, hundreds of perverts responding to a very classy personal ad, schemers, scammers, and double-dippers – she's seen them all, or bumped up against them. That was all before she met Mrs. Right, slipped on a diamond, and lived happily ever after in illegally-wedded bliss. But her picker is still in tip-top shape, so much so that her buddies regularly put their intendeds through the "AJ Test" before they get serious.

What if AJ and I you could spot the real losers before you open your life to them? What if you could see the truth about your guy or gal before the damage was done? What if you could spot the kooks before they tattoo your heart?

You *can* spot the kooks. You just need to know how.

People often ignore the whispers of doubt and explain away the warning signals all for the sake of new love. The last thing you want to believe about your lover, partner, or spouse, is that he or she is not your perfect match. Considering the notion that your sweetheart is not what he or she seems, may never change, can't love your the way you really want to be loved, or, worse, is a danger to your personal safety and financial well being, can be downright impossible.

That is, unless you know the signs.

We began this project by sharing our dating disasters, polled our friends, and then came up with a list of kooks we've known and loved. This book is our gift to all of the single (and attached) straight and gay men and women out there slogging through the dating world. It's a guide to spotting the most common "worst date" and "worst mate" personalities, the guys and gals who aren't worth your time and certainly aren't worthy of your love. In this book, you'll learn the style, motives, and strategies employed by nineteen of the worst offenders, from the benign Baby to the dangerous Control Freak.

However, this book does not include shopaholics, alcoholics, overeaters, anorexics, drug addicts, and the like because these are people with diseases of the mind, body and soul. These people are not kooks. Don't kooks have psychological problems just like drug addicts and people with eating disorders? Yes. Kooks often have complicated psychological problems that influence their kooky behavior. (Don't we all?) But if your guy or gal has a bona fide, diagnosed addiction or disorder, I would not characterize him or her as a "kook." *The American Heritage Dictionary* defines a kook as, "A person regarded as strange, eccentric, or crazy." But the word is slang, and in this book it is used to describe anyone who isn't worth wasting precious Saturday nights on.

We'll also clue you in on what you can do to protect yourself if you're just not sure that your dreamboat is really a kook, and you want to maintain the relationship. And if you're looking for new places to search for your one true love, flip to the Venue Menu at the back of the book for our take on the best ways to meet single guys and gals.

Kissing frogs is a waste of time. You need to cut straight to the chase and get on with your happily ever after. Happy pickin'!

Before you dive in, a quick note about how we approached this book:

AJ and I understand that writing from two points of view can be confusing, so we've written this entire book from a single point of view, but that point of view is collective. We've incorporated all of our shared experiences into one voice and one narrator, thereby making it easier for you, the reader, to read. In addition, we think part of what makes this book so strong is that it relates relationship mistakes and mishaps, crimes and misdemeanors that we've both made (and probably you, too). So when you read us saying, "I did this or I did that," the fact is it probably applies to both of us, which is why it doesn't matter which one of us is speaking, or writing, at that moment. We hope the singular point of view doesn't case confusion. We think it avoids it.

How to Avoid the Kooks

An ounce of kook prevention is worth a pound of therapy. Spotting kooks before they worm their way into your heart can be the difference between, "Oh well," and, "Why me?" The best protection from the kooks of the world is to make yourself undesirable to the undesirables. Here's how:

Be Authentic

The dating world is full of shape shifters and chameleons, people who change who they are to seem more appealing to the object of their affection. From their appearance to their interests to their political leanings, people alter aspects of themselves in the hopes of getting a phone number, a date, or a marriage proposal.

First of all, it's lying. We all do a little bit of it when we're trying to partner up. No woman really *wants* to wear four-inch heels all day every day or watch football for ten hours straight. No man leaps at the chance to watch his woman try on nineteen different dresses.

But the dishonesty I'm referring to goes deeper than that; it's about changing something fundamental about you in an attempt to attract and please a potential mate. You are who you are. Don't tone yourself down or make something up for anyone. When you stand in your truth, you are more apt to notice when someone is trying to feed you a line or steer you off course. When you are rooted in your own authenticity, kooks are less likely to come knockin'.

Cultivate Confidence

Kooks prey on the timid. They're not interested in someone who exudes self-confidence. A person who appears weak and insecure is more likely to let a kook in and then get away with just about anything. And I'm not talking about on-the-job confidence, the kind that got you that promotion and a company car. I'm talking about relationship confidence. Even the highest rollers can have pea-sized self-worth when it comes to affairs of the heart.

Cultivate confidence and the kooks will think twice about approaching you. How do you do that? It's easier than you think. Pretend to take yourself off the market and fill your time with creative, adventurous, and charitable endeavors.

Focus on making yourself happy rather than waiting for some nameless stranger (i.e. kook) to sort it all out for you. Expand your horizons, take chances, and learn something new. Help others, dig up childhood dreams, and take a giant bite out of life. Of course, you would like to meet the love of your life, so you're not *totally* off the market. But you're more likely to meet your dream guy or gal when you're focused on living life to the fullest. And you're LESS likely to run into kooks in the process.

Stay In the Moment

When you're dating someone, you're more likely to spot the kook if you stay completely present. Most of us (myself included) think WAY too much about the future when we're getting to know someone. It's understandable; you're sizing up the match, thinking long-term, wondering if this new dreamboat is a total waste of your time.

One of the problems with this future thinking is that it's not based in reality. The last thing you want to do is hitch up with someone's potential rather than the real person. Another downside is that the dreaming and planning distracts you from sizing up your sweetie as is. What if you miss a big red flag because you're busy reading baby name books or picking out rings? What if you're so focused on the future you can't spot the kook sitting right next to you, holding your hand?

This book will teach you how to spot some of the most common kooks around, but until you get right with yourself, you're always going to be susceptible to them. When you are genuine, confident, and rooted in the present moment, the kooks won't stand a chance.

The Agenda

Jack said that April seemed to have a deadline for getting married.

The Agendas are kooks on a mission. They seem to push through the relationship milestones quickly, as if checking them off a list. First date. Check. First kiss. Check. Confess feelings of love. Check. Suggest marriage. Check.

über goal-oriented, the Agenda usually expects a commitment by a specific date. It is not uncommon for an Agenda to give some sort of ultimatum that motivates you to throw caution to the wind. For example, she might withhold sex (I'm against sex before marriage), or threaten to cut off all contact (if this isn't going anywhere, I can't see you anymore) if she doesn't get that marriage certificate within a specific – and usually tight – timeframe.

The Agenda sees you as a means to an end, a solution to a problem. Doesn't that make your heart go pitter-patter?

Not. No matter how much Agendas profess to love you, what they really want is to either a) get out of a jam, or b) obtain something. Agenda kooks may want a green card, a father or mother for their children, a nice house to live in, a new identity, or the status marrying you would give them.

Whatever the reason, getting involved with an Agenda always leads to heartache and disillusionment. It also very often leads to financial ruin, loss of property, and nervous breakdowns – usually in that order. When you hitch your heart to the Agenda's post, you'll soon find out that his or her prize was something other than a life with you. And that discovery would break anybody's heart in two. Even yours.

It's Not About You

If you've hooked up with an Agenda, it's not about you. Let me clarify that statement further. What I'm saying really has two meanings in this case. When someone uses you for personal gain, whether that gain is status, health insurance, or something else entirely, it most certainly is not about you. In other words, it's not your fault.

But the other meaning is the one that's hard to swallow. You see, for the Agenda, it's not about you, wonderful you;

it's about what you can do for the kook. In essence, he or she is not in love with you.

The only part that *is* about you, or rather *on you*, is the part of you that acted against your better judgment. Even people who are deeply in love sign the prenup, so there's no excuse for setting aside your standards for the Agenda, or ignoring that inner voice that says, "Stop! Do not pass go! Do not collect $200!"

Even the savviest gals and smartest guys fall for Agenda kooks. But do yourself a favor and don't put anything but your heart up for grabs – ever. This goes for all kooks, including those that *might* be kooks.

But Adryenn, Don't We All Have An Agenda?

Yup, we all have an agenda. Everyone goes into new relationships with a goal on the brain. It could be as simple as getting a second date, but it's an agenda nonetheless. Once we're in a relationship, the stakes are raised. He wants marriage. She wants someone to travel the world with her. They both want a big family – right away. The agenda is the want, the images you envision, the viewfinder that focuses on your future self - your hopes, daydreams, and aspirations.

But all of those wants require a love match. Your dream gal or guy, the other half of your dynamic duo. The Agenda is not looking for love. Again, the Agenda is looking for *a means to an end*. You're just a tool, a resource; a stepping-stone to help the Agenda gets what he or she needs.

Before you go *Green Card* on me, remember that Andi MacDowell's character entered into her illegal marriage with Gérard Depardieu willingly. They met five minutes before the ceremony, and they both gained something in marrying one another. Sure, they fell in love while preparing for the Department of Immigration's test, but a) it was a movie, and b) they weren't lying to each other in order to achieve their goals.

But I KNOW About the Agenda

Your guy told you he needs a place to live when his lease is up, otherwise he'll have to move back in with his ex-wife until he can afford a place of his own. (No comment.) Maybe your gal told you right from the start that she needed to marry you so that you would not have to testify against her in her criminal case. (Again, no comment.)

Even if your gal was up front with you, or fessed up early in your relationship, that doesn't make her trustworthy – OR change the agenda. Worse, if you are prone to rescuing others or making yourself indispensable to the men in your life, this only ensures that the Agenda will reach his goal with ease, and at your expense.

We all have heard stories of two lovers torn apart by immigration laws, but this and other stories just play into our romantic notions of saving the day for our one true love. But what happens after the credits roll? Are you left single, broke, and brokenhearted?

Remember, when an Agenda enters into a commitment with you under false pretenses (i.e. he lies about loving you), there is no foundation on which to actually build a life. Even if the Agenda hangs on out of a sense of loyalty, or to further another agenda, it can only lead to mutual contempt. Because underneath it all, you know. And he or she knows you know. You're just living in a mutually agreed upon fantasy world. No matter how much fun they're all having, they all have to wave goodbye to Mr. York and Tattoo and get on that plane.

Why Do Agendas Do It?

There could be a whole host of reasons why Agenda kooks choose to use another human being to solve a problem rather than handle it on their own. Poor self-esteem, or fear of facing their problems, or a very shaky grip on reality, for example.

The world is full of opportunists, and these people really never change. Opportunists are very often also narcissists, and there's no talking sense to them – they're too busy talking to their own reflection to notice. Some have had to learn to be an opportunist because of circumstance. Perhaps they grew up in poverty and learned fast how to size others up to see what they could do for them. Maybe they learned from example, from a parent or role model who practiced opportunism as a way of life.

Whatever the reason, Agendas cannot be cured of their kookiness. And even if they could be cured, you're not man or woman enough to do it. This takes a divine revelation that allows the Agenda to gain an empathic nature, followed by years of cognitive behavioral therapy. Who's got time for that?

It Must Be Love (Or Why YOU Do It)

It was a whirlwind romance. I was swept off my feet. It was love at first sight. Sound familiar? It should. That's how relationships very often play out in the movies, on television, and in those ubiquitous drugstore romance novels. In these stories, love is fast, passionate, and instantly life-altering. Look, I'm not saying this type of experience doesn't genuinely happen; I just want you to consider the fact that you *may* be influenced by a few stories you *may or may not have* seen, read, or heard.

Don't kick yourself for getting caught up in the moment. A new romance makes us feel alive and on track and superhuman. And when the Agenda comes at you with no reservations, no hesitation to commit, it seems that you have found "the one" at last. This kook conjures up a thrilling experience paired with definitive declarations, and that's almost impossible to refuse.

But do consider the possibility that you may be more susceptible to the Agenda, and kooks in general, because you feel there's something missing from your life. Why are you so willing to dive into this relationship? What void is this kook filling? Or do you think this is your last chance for happiness? (Trust me: It's not.)

How to Spot the Agenda

Not all Agendas are easy to spot because it is usually in their best interest to keep their agenda from you as long as they can. I know of a man who, in his late fifties, dated a woman with four kids, a minivan, and two properties in a small town. They met in November. By January, she was redecorating his house. By May, they were married. He wondered why she wanted to be married by May, but because she was withholding sex from him (for religious reasons), and because she seemed to be independent with her own job and assets, he went for it.

In June, the balloon payments on her two properties came due, and the minivan broke down. This newlywed was out $100,000 plus in his first month of marriage, and it's been downhill ever since. He now supports her, her four children (three are over eighteen), her mother, and her grandmother. Heck of a deal, right?

There are some basic signs that can help you spot an Agenda, no matter how slick she is at covering her tracks. Here are a few warning signs that, if present in your guy or gal, pretty much guarantee you have hooked up with an Agenda (or some other kook):

- **Always in a Rush**

Though you may not know the reason behind the rush, the Agenda is always in a big hurry. Hurry up and go on a date, hurry up and express his or her undying love, hurry up and move in or get married and move in, and hurry up and sign on the dotted line.

All of this rushing about may feel exciting to you at first, as if you've finally found that fairy-tale romance everyone keeps talking about. But at the back of your mind there is that nagging sense of doubt. The little ping that sounds like an alarm clock that won't quit.

Why does she have to get married so fast? Why can't he wait for that April wedding I've been planning since I was ten years old? Why do we have to move to California to get married? (Hint on that one: community property, Baby).

When you ignore the little voice that says, "Hold up," you are putting yourself at great risk. That little voice is not cold feet; it's your own survival instincts kicking in.

- **Too Agreeable**

Isn't it amazing how everything you do, say, and believe is A-OK with your honey? If you can do no wrong, even if you *know* you did wrong, you have to ask yourself if you have an Agenda biting his tongue while he bides his time.

We're all golden in the early days of love, but there is always some conflict that rises up eventually. A new relationship is all about working out the kinks to see if you're compatible. The Agenda doesn't want to face any kinks for fear that you may determine she is not the one. So if you're irking her in some way, you're not going to hear about it.

- **Makes No Plans Beyond D-Day**

While the Agenda is big on making plans, there is often a cutoff point, a time period that he or she seems reluctant to discuss. It may be the day after your wedding or much later, but there is a cutoff point. If you think about it for a little while, you'll come up with it. Perhaps he avoids any discussion about that cruise you want to take next year. Or maybe she changes the subject when you make out your Christmas list.

Test the waters. Push the issue. If your guy or gal still refuses to look beyond D-Day – whatever that day represents – you've got a problem.

- **Doesn't Like Your Friends and Family**

If your guy or gal finds fault with your family, or seems to steer you away from seeing your friends, you most definitely have a kook on your hands. While your family may give *The Addams Family* a run for its money, a true new love is not going to tear your family down. It's bad form. And your friends? Those are the people she should be trying to win over with beer, flattery, and good deeds.

Isolating you from your nearest and dearest is a tactic used by all sorts of kooks, some of them more dangerous than others. The Agenda benefits because you are less likely to have a heart-to-heart with a concerned love one, who straight up tells you how it really is with your guy or gal.

Keeping you separate from those close to you by whatever means is a sure sign you've got yourself a kook.

- **Things Just Don't Add Up**

Not all Agenda kooks are con artists. Some are just in difficult situations looking for a way out and have very little practice pulling the wool over someone's eyes. Most Agendas will trip up, forget the details of their stories, and then tell them again with a different beginning, middle or end.

Think about it, and think hard. Does everything add up? Has your guy or gal told you something that doesn't ring true? Have you come across any papers or (accidentally) overheard any conversations that make you feel as though she is keeping something from you?

If you've been accepting flimsy explanations and filling in the blanks on your own so that you don't have to face reality, it's time to stop. Be your own detective and find out what's really going on before it's too late. A word about the warning signs: not every Agenda will have all of these signs. Some Agenda kooks plan to stick around for years to achieve a lofty goal such as fat alimony checks or a free education. Likewise, not all Agenda kooks are sweet as pie; they use meanness to get what they want. And some Agendas will fit in great with your family, too.

BUT, if your guy or gal is in a rush to get hitched (or move in, or hook up), that is the most important warning sign of all. Don't ignore it or think it's romantic or cute. Question, question, question – until you get the truth.

What if I'm Not Sure?

If you're still not sure if your honey bunch is an Agenda, but you're not ready to believe him or her wholeheartedly, either, it would be best to take some steps to protect yourself. Here are my recommendations for the *minimum* you should do if you suspect you're involved with an Agenda:

Do Your Homework

If you're still wondering if your guy or gal is on the up and up, it's time to don your P.I. cap and get to work. But before you go snooping around, ask to see the papers: driver's license, green card (if applicable), social security card, bank statements, credit card statements, and any lease, loan, and mortgage documents. If your sweetie is reluctant to show you these documents, or stalls indefinitely, you pretty much know you have a kook on your hands-- maybe not an Agenda but still a kook, probably of a different stripe.

If you are brave, dig around a bit to find these documents on your own. A quick look will probably tell you all that you need to know. If you'd rather not be the one to find the dirt your guy or gal, hire a private investigator to do it for you. An experienced, legitimate investigator can find out almost anything you need to know, and fast. Isn't your future worth a little recon?

Hold Off on Everything

If you are even the tiniest bit concerned that you may have fallen for an Agenda, hold off on any plans you may have made. If you're nervous about giving your sweetie a reason for the wait, just say you, "Need more time to get used to the idea," or something vague and hard to argue with but not hurtful.

Whatever you do, do not get married, sign a lease, a contract, a loan, a credit card application or anything else with this person until you are absolutely sure she does not have ulterior motives in courting you.

Protect Your Assets

If you're not married and don't live with your guy or gal, your assets are pretty well protected. Living together can complicate things, especially if you have lived together long enough to be considered "common law" married. (The number of years varies from state to state.) But if you are already married, or are planning to get married, you need to take the following steps to protect your assets:

1. Get a lawyer and then get a prenup. After you're married, get a postnup to seal the deal.
2. Designate a beneficiary on your life insurance and retirement accounts who is not your fiancé/spouse but someone you can trust.
3. Keep your own bank account, separate from your sweetie.
4. Keep your records private.
5. Make a list of all of your possessions and assets.

All of us want to believe that the person we love is not after money, property, status, citizenship, or reproductive abilities. We want to believe that our beloved wants to be with us so badly, he or she will sidestep all of the usual steps to marriage, never realizing that we are being asked to sidestep as well.

If you have hooked up with an Agenda, get out, and get out fast. No tearful goodbyes, no second chances. Cold turkey is the only way. Otherwise, your Agenda kook may get what he wants before you get the nerve up to finally cut and run. And by then, he or she will be long gone.

The Baby

Suzie said Gerald had no idea how to take care of himself and expected her to do his laundry, cooking, and shopping.

Like infants, the Baby is an irresistible kook. At first. The adorable naiveté, the vulnerability, the need for your attention and guidance. Our parental instincts kick in, and just as we coo and smile at newborns, we giggle and swell around these seemingly innocent kooks. But the Baby is a lot smarter than you think he or she is. In fact, Baby may be smarter than you.

Though this kook appears to be a clean slate just waiting for a partner of your experience to rescue him or her from glaring ineptitude, the Baby is actually a master of manipulation. He's the guy who claims to have no knowledge of how to handle money and expects you to manage all of his finances. She's the gal who looks blankly at the vacuum as if she has never seen one before in her life. She's the kook that expects you to pick her up from work every day, so she doesn't have to take the scary bus. He's the guy who, when you have him over for a romantic dinner, brings his laundry and expects you to do it for him.

The Baby is the likable kook who seems trainable, so we dive in with both hands and get to work. She just needs a few cooking lessons, or a little more confidence so she can order takeout on her own. Wrong. Although at first she may seem willing to learn at your feet, this kook actually has no intention of becoming self-sufficient. And why should she? What possible motivation would the Baby have to give up a life of dependence for the busy, exhausting, irritating life of an independent person? You (or the parents, ex-lovers, friends) are taking care of everything for this kook.

As long as you keep it up, he's not going to lift a finger to change, no matter how hard you cry or how often you complain. And if the day ever comes when you finally throw in the towel, don't expect the Baby to wise up and win you back. The Baby will always be a baby, and he will have no trouble finding another willing partner to hold his hand through life. So do you want to be the parent, or are you willing to let this one go?

The Charming Incompetent

It's cute how your sweetie can't program the VCR. You like it when she asks you to come over and kill a spider (yeah, I know, *Annie Hall*). You love to tell your friends how your guy will eat only your cooking (except for Mom's, but she lives in Florida, so that doesn't count).

In the beginning of your love affair with the Baby, the incompetence seems charming. You feel sorry for your muffin, wondering why he never learned how to sew a button or parallel park. There's a smile on your face as you iron the basket of shirts he brought over after work. Your heart beats faster as you take her car in for an oil change. You *like* taking care of the Baby. Never before have you felt so needed, so important, so…essential.

The Baby gets away with it, because of that disarming, "help me" smile and those big doe eyes. He seals the deal by expressing gratitude in really lovely ways, like flowers, kisses, praise, and a few steamy things we won't mention (I want you to focus, okay?).

When you first hook up with a Baby, she is appreciative and accommodating. Oh, you can't walk my dog at 4:00 because you have a meeting? Would you be able to come at 6:00 instead? If it's inconvenient to call the phone company for me today, would you mind doing it tomorrow? She still gets her favor but on your terms, so you feel in control. Almost as if you said, "No." Which you didn't. You said, "Yes," every time.

This kook just oozes charm and innocence, and so you whistle while you work. In fact, the Baby is so enchanting that you don't even notice that he or she hasn't offered to do one thing for you the entire time you've been together. If those needy ways get to you now and again, you just shake your head and let it roll of your back because it can't go on forever, right? At some point Baby will have to pitch in and figure it out. Right? Sure. Whatever you say.

Does Dish Soap Work in the Washing Machine?

Once a Baby evolves from a fling to a steady, Baby gets more creative. Rather than simply ask you for help, he or she now resorts to totally screwing things up so you have to do it yourself or live with the consequences of the incompetence. She wants to get out of doing the laundry, so she deliberately washes your red sweater with the white towels, and presto! - You're doing the laundry for the next century. He doesn't feel like dealing with the bills, so he wreaks havoc on your finances by transferring all of your money to your savings account after writing checks to all of your creditors. Shock of all shocks, you've taken the checkbook away from him and he's free of any financial responsibility for the rest of your (un)happy life together.

You see, it takes smarts to remain a virtual child for all of your adult life. The Babies know that in order for them to get out of grown-up responsibilities, they will have to find someone else for the job. While you may be more than willing to do his holiday shopping or stand in line for her at the DMV when you're first hitting the sheets, at some point you will grow tired of it and start complaining. That's when the Babies change tactics and show you just how inept they "really" are.

All of a sudden, your guy or gal is the clumsiest, ditziest person on earth. When it comes to drying dishes, he's all thumbs (goodbye complete set of Depression-era dessert plates); she's clueless about tire pressure (*sayonara* $300 tires). The Babies get out of everything by first trying it and then failing miserably. They do everything badly, very badly, so you'll "just do it" to get them to STOP trying. And they will. Anything to make you happy, Honey. You know best.

Great Expectations

Act three in the saga of you and the kook is a bit depressing, I'm afraid. Gone is the sweet guy or gal that fell over backwards to praise you for your good deeds. No longer are you a willing volunteer receiving applause and gratitude. The Baby has morphed into a whiny, insolent person who is alternately demanding and distant.

Rather than ask you to pack her gym bag, she now gets angry if you forget to do it automatically. Don't you care about her? Don't you realize she'll be late for yoga – again! Instead of thanking you for a wonderful meal, he now eats in front of the TV and wonders when you'll make something other than chicken. As long as you're up, will you get me a beer? And some chips? And a blanket for my feet?

The Baby is now an overgrown toddler with no intention of changing. Your helpful tasks are no longer favors, they are requirements of the job--a thankless position that exhausts you emotionally and physically and leaves little room for your own self-care. Just like you dreamed it would be, isn't it?

Why Do Babies Do It?

Why does the Baby act like such a...baby? I have three words for you: because Baby can! The Baby is a baby because it's easy to pull off. After all, there are so many willing parties. It's likely that these kooks had a childhood free of chores and responsibilities, with parents that cleaned up after them and bailed them out of jams.

For whatever reason, the Babies had parents that didn't want them to grow up and so neglected an important component of parenting: teaching their children to be independent. Likewise, your sweetie may have witnessed a household in which one parent took care of everything and the other...didn't. In essence, the Baby learned how to be a Baby by watching a parent act like one.

Babies need parents, or a nanny, to help them get through the day, so it's likely your guy or gal found a few of them along the way. There's a good chance that your Baby has a few ex-mommies or ex-daddies disguised as former flames, partners that enabled the behavior to continue right up until the day you met. It is possible to go through life never having to fend for yourself. And if anyone can pull it off, it's the Baby.

What Would I Do Without You? (Or Why YOU Do It)

Loving a Baby can be very gratifying for some people. It fills a need to be needed; to be needed so much, there is no way this kook is letting you go. To some extent, we all like to be needed. We want to be seen as important and valued by our partners. But if you've settled down with a Baby it might be partly because his or her need for you fills your *own need* to be needed. To be indispensable.

This kook can often be found in vulnerable situations, such as stranded by the side of the road, or helplessly searching for rock salt in the spice aisle. We are drawn to these kooks in part because we get to rescue them in some capacity.

Soon we come to the Baby's aid in small ways every day. You get to be the white knight to her distressed damsel or his lost boy, and there is something alluring about that. If you get a larger-than-average charge out of rescuing your friends and lovers, you are a prime candidate for the next Mr. or Mrs. Baby. Because as long as you are getting something from the exchange, you are more likely to sign up for the job – permanently.

If your partner is constantly abdicating to you, that puts you "in charge." The illusion of control is intoxicating and could be another reason why you find the Baby so tempting. Being with this kook also seems to expand your sphere of influence, allowing you to mold your lover into the "perfect" partner. You start thinking it's actually a *good* thing that he or she can't make a bed. Now you can teach your sweetie how to do it *exactly* the way you like it! Sounds good to me. But no matter how many times you teach the Baby to do something, Baby will forget, or flub it up, or just stop trying altogether. The point is to get *you* to keep doing it. Remember?

Whether you fell for this kook because you have a subconscious desire to be indispensable, to be a mommy or daddy, to rescue someone, to control the relationship, or to mentor your lover, the Baby is filling a deep need in you.

The Baby knows this about you and, just to make sure, presents you with a simple test to prove it. The first task Baby asks you to perform because Baby can't, won't, or doesn't have a clue how to is the first test to determine if you will fit the Baby's requirements for a partner. How'd you do? Pass or fail?

How to Spot the Baby

Because the Babies have a laundry list of responsibilities that they can't seem to handle, these kooks have set up their lives in such a way that they never have to try. One sure way to spot the Babies is to look at the living arrangements. By that I mean not only where they live but also *how* they live. Here are a few common kooky Baby setups:

- **Still Living With Mom**

In order to get out of most every household responsibility, the Baby opts to hang at the homestead well into adulthood. Babies are also often home-hoppers, running back to Mommy and Daddy when a live-in relationship doesn't work out. Babies may also be two kooks in one (double your pleasure!) - a Baby and a Loafer. If Babies are both, I'm certain they still live at home, and probably never left.

Even if your sweetie has his own place, he still may get what he needs by spending a lot - I mean *a lot* - of time with Mom and Dad. Your sweetie's parents might do his laundry, take care of her pets, move in when he's sick, fix meals for her freezer, and wrap *your* birthday present. Remember, these are all things that YOU will end up doing when Baby moves in with you.

- **Camps Out at Your Place**

  If the Baby isn't living at Mom's and Dads, she is likely camped out at your place. The Baby doesn't like to spend a lot of time alone because that would mean that she might have to take out the trash, look for the remote, and pick up the dry cleaning. By staying over at your place most nights, this kook makes it easier for you to "do your job." Since you're doing your own laundry, could you just throw in a few of my things? You're stopping by the store before you get home? Why don't you just pick up the stuff on my list, too, and save me a trip?

Another bonus to spending a ton of time at your place is the Baby can claim that she can't find anything, doesn't know how to work anything, and wouldn't want to put anything back in the wrong place. It's your house, and so you get to do the work. You do it so well, anyway. She'd just mess it up.

- **Backed By a Team of Professionals**

If none of the above is true, you might be smiling now, thinking your instincts were totally wrong and you have not hooked up with a Baby. Ahem. I'm not done yet. Even if your guy has his own place and spends plenty of time there, he may still be a Baby; he's just not making you the parent – yet.

If your dreamboat is a Baby, you can be sure someone is doing for your sweetie what he refuses to do for himself. This kook may have a team of people at his beck and call, taking care of every last detail, so that he can be a Baby and yet appear to be successful and together.

He may have a housekeeper, a cook or meal delivery, a dog walker, a therapist, and an assistant on payroll. On the upside, it does take a certain amount of cash to pull this off, so at least you won't have to pay for everything, too. But a Baby is a Baby is a Baby. I call 'em as I see 'em. (Besides, don't think that when you're married, many of these hired hands won't magically disappear and leave you holding the laundry bag!)

What if I'm Not Sure?

I'll give you the benefit of the nagging doubt. Your sweetie may simply have lived a sheltered life and is really more than willing to learn how to break free from dependence on others. Well, there's one way to find out! Here are three strategies that may help you identify this kook once and for all and help you move on to taking care of the person that matters most: you.

- **Time to Grow Up**

As every parent knows, sometimes tough love is the only and best option. Time to give that to-do list back to your princess and watch how she reacts. Challenge your gal to take on all of the responsibilities she has been avoiding, not just one or two. State your case, letting her know that you want to be interdependent, not codependent, or you may have to move on. Stop being the parent, and if your gal still refuses to grow up, she's a Baby for sure.

- **Some Assistance, Please?**

If the first strategy seems too harsh, start by asking for help with your own tasks and see what happens. It may be that your guy enjoys leaning on you but would also be happy to return the favor. Make a list of tasks you would like help with and go through them one at a time. Approach your prince, asking for his help with something other than a task he asked you to do.

If you get the same routine you always get, try again. Explain that you have too much on your plate and could really use a hand. Let your guy know that taking care of his responsibilities has caused you to come up short on your own tasks, and you need help to pull it all off. If he still says, "No" or finds a way to wriggle out of it, cut your losses. A guy who continues to be dead weight is definitely a Baby.

- **Life 101**

If neither of these approaches is your style, why not suggest she begin the process of becoming independent. Explain your concerns, especially the long-term consequences of living with a Baby, and request that she learn how to fend for herself so that you can stay together and build a life.

Perhaps she needs to take a basic cooking class, or attend a personal finance seminar, or find a life coach to help connect all of the dots. Whatever your partner needs to learn, make sure you are not the teacher. This role is not healthy, sexy, or fun. Have your sweetie find someone else to show her the way, and then step back and let it happen.

Remember, if your beloved does agree to grow up and get educated, he or she may come out of it with a different approach than you. Whatever you do, DO NOT criticize when a former Baby finally does learn how to take care of things. Be grateful that Baby's no longer a kook, and leave it at that.

By partnering with the Baby, you become the parent. His or her parent provides everything a baby needs. *Everything.* So, if it turns out that your sweetie is a Baby-variety of kook, it means you are ultimately responsible for everything, too. A Baby only gets more dependent over time, which means you will get more frustrated, tired, and angry. It's like that old adage, "Give them an inch and they take a mile."

If you're in love with a Baby and can't see the way out of it just yet, please take a moment to look at your own self-care. Are you getting what you need? Have you put off going to the gym, the doctor, or the therapist because you are too busy taking care of this kook? Do you see your old friends and visit your old haunts, at least once in a while? What about your interests and passions? When was the last time you took time out for you?

The Baby cannot provide you with the same level of support you are dishing out, and so at the very least, start providing it for yourself. Most Babies will be annoyed by your efforts to improve your own self-care, but by that time, you will feel better about everything and more willing to face the truth. The truth that you deserve more, so much more. And as long as your hitched up to the Baby, you'll never get it.

The Big Spender

Laura said she rarely sees Dave anymore, but she has an exquisite collection of Bulgari jewelry.

Life with the Big Spender has its perks. Couture clothing, luxury cars, fine wine, and exotic vacations. This kook is all about cash and what it can buy. Which isn't such a bad thing, if you like stuff and enjoy the high life. But the thing that makes these kooks so kooky is they think they can buy *you*, too.

Don't get me wrong. I'm not saying you're for sale, per se. But the Big Spender *thinks* you are, to some extent. The Big Spender uses expensive gifts and experiences to woo you, appease you when you're angry, apologize for his or her transgressions and, if necessary, win you back. On paper, saying, "No," to a Big Spender seems like the obvious choice. But faced with a brightly wrapped peace offering, you may find it impossible to cut this kook loose.

Again, I'm not suggesting you're a materialistic, shallow person with no personal integrity. I'm saying the Big Spender is a materialistic, shallow person with no personal integrity. But if you've already fallen in love with one of these types, and the kook presents you with a lovely token to make amends for forgetting your anniversary or, say, missing your big speech to the U.N., you are predisposed to welcome the gift and forget all about the diss.

The Big Spender may be fun to be around at first, and you may feel a bit like a kid in a candy store. The Big Spender lives large, which means you get to live large, too. Despite the fact that your relationship is based on cool friends and hot times, you keep thinking you'll get to know the real person behind this upwardly mobile, stuff-loving success story. You'll get to see him or her cry, hear a formative story or two, or share a private moment that bonds you forever. Nope. The Big Spender doesn't do intimacy because there's nothing there. Scratch beneath the surface, and you'll find he or she is really full of...hot air.

So if you're content to hang on the arm of the Big Spender, accepting gifts instead of love, by all means welcome this kook with open arms. But if you want more from your partner than a primo bag of swag, it's time to return this kook to sender!

Sure My Lover's Materialistic, But...

My guy is a megawatt mogul, why shouldn't he buy me a co-op on the Upper East Side? My gal bought me a prized racehorse, but so what, she's loaded! Let me be perfectly clear: I am not talking about rich people who love their toys and like to spread the love around. I'm talking about kooks who use money to buy their way in – and out – of relationships, kooks who let money do all of the talking, fixing, and apologizing.

If your guy simply likes to buy stuff, who am I to call him a kook? If your gal is wonderful to you in every way, cares about your feelings, shows up for dates, and seems groovy in every other way, who am I to call her a kook just because she indulges in a little consumerism, and perhaps a glass of pretension, now and then? I may not want to date a snob, but if your snob is the best partner you've ever had, I wouldn't classify him or her as a kook.

Do you see the distinction? Big Spenders are not capable of having a healthy relationship, because they use money as a substitute for love, companionship, and intimacy. They are shallow puddles of a person. You want a deep ocean of a person, a rushing river, an expansive lake. After all, a puddle dries up pretty fast, and then all you're left with is a patch of mud.

But Adryenn, My Sweetie's Just a Shopaholic!

I hear you. You're trying valiantly to convince me that your guy or gal really isn't a Big Spender at all but rather just simply has a shopping addiction. Nice. Well, it could be true. Your sweetie may not be a kook at all, just a person who needs professional help to overcome compulsive spending. Which is worse? Only you can be judge.

An out-of-control spending habit may be the reason behind the gifts you receive instead of love, but I doubt it. Shopaholics are in it for the rush, the high from spending and buying, despite potentially disastrous consequences. The Big Spender gives gifts, cash, and good times in lieu of intimacy and honesty. Both the Big Spender and the Shopaholic need professional help, no doubt, but it's important to create a distinction between the two. One just has a problem with spending; the other has a problem connecting. Got it?

Bought and Paid For

Let's take a walk into the future, shall we? What will life be like married to a Big Spender? Do you see a life filled with silly pillow fights and tender moments, your partner standing at your side as you win, fall, leap, and crash? Or do you see a life filled with stuff, stuff, and more stuff, with you wandering around a big empty house all by your lonesome?

The Big Spender may shower you with gifts to win your heart, or to repair the relationship and move it forward, but by the time you've sealed the deal, Mr. or Mrs. Big Spender views you as "bought and paid for." It's a common problem in all marriages, no matter the income level. People stop trying to delight their partner to keep them glowing from the inside out. But while most of us recognize that we need to nurture our marriages, the Big Spender sees no reason to waste his or her precious energy or time on this nurturing nonsense. After all, you signed on the dotted line. What more is there to do?

Within the marriage, you may still receive a Rolex or a spa trip to Cabo, but the Big Spender doesn't have to try as hard to keep you happy. Eventually, you're so tied to your Big Spender lifestyle that you can't figure out how to extricate yourself. All of your friends run in the same circles, your kids go to the best private schools, and you can't remember why you were in college in the first place. You're stuck. Bought and paid for.

Why Do Big Spenders Do It?

For whatever reason unique to your sweetie, the Big Spender is incapable of an intimate connection with you. It could be because your guy learned this behavior from his parents or had a profoundly negative experience that prevented him from being vulnerable. Or it could be that she measures her own worth with money, stuff, prestige, and success and values it above all else. Even you.

Because the Big Spenders can't – or won't – connect with you, they use gifts as a stand in. Rather than feel humble, acknowledge your feelings, or bond with you in any way other than physically, the Big Spenders opt to let expensive offerings speak on their behalf. He misses your birthday, and you receive an amazing belated present designed to erase any memory of the transgression. She accepts a date from another man, and you receive a beautifully wrapped treasure instead of an explanation or a heartfelt apology.

It's not a new concept, really. Throughout history people have given gifts as gestures, allowing the gift to express what is in their heart or on their agenda. In Victorian times, each type of gift, down to the different blooms in a bouquet of flowers, represented a specific emotion and desire. Gift giving was an intricate, meaningful art, borne of a time when the concept of being "in love" was newly in fashion.

But for the Big Spender, generosity is not from the heart. It's a necessary expense, like paying the cleaning lady or having the car detailed. Somewhere in the Big Spender's mind is a list of monthly expenses, and you're on it. Pay gardener. Tip doorman. Keep lover happy.

Again, the exact reasons why your Big Spender developed into a shallow, empty shell of a person are beyond me. (They're probably beyond you, too.) But it really doesn't matter. You can't teach a self-serving kook how to put you first, no matter how hard you try. *No matter how hard you try.*

Blinded by the Bling (or Why YOU Do It)

Okay, you don't want to admit it, but you like the bling. You enjoy showing off your new Cartier tennis bracelet, and you can't wait to try out the new Bose sound system. Everybody, especially Americans, loves having stuff. More. Bigger. Better. New. That's cool. I like my gadgets as much as the next person. But I don't let stuff serve as a substitute for thoughtfulness, kindness, or respect in my marriage.

Gifts also hold significant meaning and so can carry you through the tough times. Wearing your boyfriend's letter jacket as you wind your way through the halls of your high school somehow takes the sting out of the fact that you weren't invited to the "biggest party of the year." Just looking at the ring your girlfriend gave you before she left for Spain, comforts you when you miss her most.

More than just love of having stuff, we like *getting* stuff. We like the process of receiving a gift. It's exciting, hopeful, and it makes you feel special. You matter. You count. You are important.

If you get a charge out of getting gifts and having stuff, well, you're just like everyone else I know – including me. But if you attach an unhealthy value to receiving and having, it might explain why you tolerate the Big Spender in your life. Perhaps your father was away a lot on business and always made up for it by returning with a fantastic present. Maybe your birthday was the only day of the year you felt special.

Before you can cut the Big Spender loose, you'll first have to examine why you like this kook in the first place. In many ways, facing the truth about yourself will be harder than facing the truth about your kook.

How to Spot the Big Spender

Lucky for you, the Big Spender is easy to spot. Well-groomed, sporting the best of everything, the Big Spender usually sticks out a like sore thumb. This kook has money and likes to throw it around. You'll notice the kook right away, but will you see the Big Spender for what he or she truly is? Since this kook's qualities are obvious, I've created a list of telltale signs for those of you that are already enmeshed with a Big Spender. Ask yourself these important questions, and then see where you stand:

- **Are You Lonely?**

Do you find yourself waiting for your honey pie, who is sometimes hours late? Do you spend a lot of time alone, because sweetie is busy with "important" work commitments? When you do spend time together, do you find that a good part of it is focused on acquiring something? Does your mate prefer to spend time with you only within a group?

If you're in love and spend most of your time alone surrounded by tokens of your sweetie's affection, you may be involved with a Big Spender. Even if you see your lover often enough to feel okay about it all, you may still get that lonely feeling when you're together. While there could be other reasons why you feel lonely in your relationship, feeling disconnected or overlooked by your partner could mean you found yourself a kook.

- **Do You Recognize Yourself?**

Do you ever step outside of yourself for a moment and look at your life with awe and sadness? Do you feel uncomfortable in your surroundings or in your newfound role? Do you look back fondly on simpler times, when you were more focused on friendship, fun, love, and community? Would you trade all of your best stuff for an honest, heartfelt conversation with your partner? Do you fantasize about kidnapping your sweetie to a faraway beach or forest, free of cell phones and ATM machines? When you look in the mirror, do you recognize yourself?

Over time, the life we created for ourselves is pushed aside to make room for our new love, the Big Spender. Why? Because Big Spenders take up too much space, change the rules, and require infinite compromise. The Big Spender can lead even the strongest souls down the path of least resistance because we want to be patient, kind, and understanding. Because we want to be loved.

When we fall in love with a non-kook, there's still plenty of negotiation. Our lives are *supposed* to look different when we merge with another. But a nurturing relationship built on mutual respect and love does not require people to render themselves unrecognizable. After all, didn't your partner fall in love with *you*, not some modified version of you that succumbs to his or her every whim? Oh. Right. Your partner's a kook. Never mind.

- **What Do You Stand For?**

Do you find yourself nodding in agreement to opinions that last month would have annoyed you? Do you have more tolerance for people or views that previously disgusted you? Do you make excuses for your new friends, in the presence of your old friends? Have you stopped speaking up in the presence of your sweetie? Did you wake up one morning and wonder where you'd left your standards?

Slowly but surely, loving the Big Spender will require you to hack away at your well-earned set of values, so that there is nothing left but what fits with his or her way of life. At first, you may think you can change your Big Spender's mind about this or that through careful illumination and smart repartee. But the Big Spender just smiles and nods, and you start to feel just a little naïve. Or the Big Spender argues with you vehemently, and you finally give up in order to make peace and, hopefully, make out.

In order to create a life with a Big Spender, you will either have to shut up or change. Because you won't change this kook. Big Spender's never give up and never change their minds *because they're never wrong.* After all, if what they thought about anything was so wrong, then how did they end up with all this money to spend on you? This is America: if you've got money, you must be doing something right. The Big Spender's ego is a driving force that is much stronger than your love, and in the end, it will always win.

What if I'm Not Sure?

I get it. You hit the love jackpot. Gorgeous, fun, funny, smart, and rich all in one package. Let's face it; even if your sweetie has just two of those qualities, you've hit pay dirt. I'm guessing if you're still reading this chapter, you are 99.9% sure you're in deep with a Big Spender. But you're holding out on the off chance that he or she will see the light and, like Bill Murray in *Scrooged*, ditch his greedy, success-at-all-costs mentality and come to appreciate your job at the homeless shelter. Okay. If you *really* want to know if there's hope for your love, try BOTH of these tips on your guy or gal and carefully note the response:

- **No Gifts, Please**

Establish a rule that you cannot give each other any gifts for six weeks (or longer, if you can hold out). This is an all-out boycott on gift giving, including last minute trinkets. It also means you cannot buy gifts and hold on to them until the boycott is over. No gifts. Period.

During the six weeks, pay attention to how your partner handles conflict between you, how wrongs are righted and devotion is expressed. Can she do it without the stuff? Is he able to communicate with you using words and actions rather than diamonds and DVDs?

- **The Gift that Keeps on Giving**

Once the six-week gift boycott is up, it's time for phase two: giving from the heart. Establish a new rule that requires both of you to give only gifts that you a) made yourself, or b) are found objects, or c) are donations made in your partner's name.

I do not recommend setting a time limit on this because, frankly, it's just a good rule. With this rule in place, the focus is on each other rather than stuff. It allows you to express your affection in a meaningful way. Plus, you save money. Tons of it. And as you know, I'm all about that.

For new lovers, it's a freakin' great rule. Why? Because you're all about the mushy, heartfelt sentiments at this stage in the game. You'll have no trouble conjuring up creative handmade cards, knitting sweaters, and baking cookies from scratch for birthdays, thank-yous, and all of those mini-anniversaries new couples enjoy celebrating (first kiss, first date, first smoothie...).

If your sweetie is totally against this rule, it could be that he is a bit lazy or feels uninspired or put on the spot. But it could also be that she is a Big Spender who has no intention of changing her ways. Which is it? Hmmm.

What's wrong with a little token of affection? Nothing. Absolutely nothing. But by now you've figured out that the Big Spender uses gifts to make up for his or her own inadequacies and generally keep you in line. If you feel good about the gift, it's probably a harmless gesture of love from a well-meaning sweetie. If you feel a bit uneasy about receiving the gifts, or eventually look at the gifts with resentment, it's likely you're hung up on a kook.

Remember this about the Big Spenders: They view everything as replaceable. Your car broke down? Your television won't work? Your laptop fizzled out in the first month? Just go out and get a new one. What's the big deal? My friend, this attitude applies to you, too. More. Bigger. Better. New. So, are you ready to cut and run?

The Buddy

Zoe said in more than six months of "dating" Parker, he had yet to officially ask her out.

You have fun together. You have great sex. You see each other all of the time. But you're starting to feel like maybe this mattress magician doesn't view your relationship in the same way you do. Maybe, just maybe, your one and only sees you as a good friend, rather than a long-term love.

The Buddies are beguiling kooks because they send so many mixed signals you end up spending all of your off time trying to figure them out. Remember junior high school? It's like that. Passing notes in class asking, "But do you think he *likes me*, likes me?" I'm going to tell you what your best friends won't: if you have to ask, the answer is, "No."

While you harbor a fantasy about long-term love, the Buddy has no plans for you past Saturday night. In fact, you may even be Saturday's Plan B. The Buddy is the guy that calls you late at night to "come over" (can you say, booty call?). She's the gal who calls only when she needs something (can you say, user?). The Buddy is the person who asks you if you want to "hang out" rather than "go out." Frequently at your place, the Buddy rarely – if ever – stays the night and absolutely never stays for breakfast.

Sound familiar? If you think the Buddy sounds a lot like a cheater, you're right. This kook *is* cheating you – cheating you out of a real, loving relationship with long-term potential. Even if your Buddy is not dating or sleeping with someone else (yeah, right), he or she is playing you for sure. This kook knows the rules of the game and knows you want the real deal. So the Buddy strings you along to get what he or she wants from you. Companionship. Sex. Stuff. Money. More sex. Help with chores. Advice. Did I mention sex? So this Buddy of yours isn't your leading man or lady. Worse, Buddy's not much of a friend. (Would you let your *real* buddies play you like this?)

So, let's review. He's not a lover (bed buddies don't count). She's not a friend (liars don't count). What's left? Easy. He or she is a kook. A fraud. A *Buddy*. So don't wait up. Turn off your phone. Get on with your life. You deserve the real thing.

Friends, with Benefits

Not all Buddies start out as kooks. Many are born of bed-buddy agreements, wherein both of you profess to not want a romantic relationship, and then one of you develops said romantic feelings over time. But the other one doesn't. In order to maintain the relationship "as is," this person becomes a Buddy. He or she skirts the issue, avoids intimacy, and starts to keep his or her distance – and secrets – all to hold on to you, the friend with benefits. Why not? It's a great deal. Until one of you falls in love.

Bruce Lee said, "Love is like friendship caught on fire." It's a beautiful sentiment, and it's true. Some of the most passionate love affairs – and the best marriages – began as a friendship and evolved into a romantic relationship. We are surrounded by stories of lovers who were friends first, both real stories and those made-up for our viewing pleasure. We know that it's possible for a friendship to grow into something more, and so we hold out for it.

Is it possible your "friend" feels the same way you do and would like to take your friendship to the next level? Sure it is. Might you wake up one day to find your "friend" standing over you with flowers and a hand-written confession of love? It could happen. But before you close this book and go back to your daydreaming ways, take a few moments to figure out how to spot this kook. Not all friends are created equal, and some are Buddies in disguise.

Romance is for Lovers

Just because you're having sex doesn't mean you're lovers. Okay, technically it does mean that. But not emotionally. The guy who swaps skin with you and then refers to you as his "friend" is not your lover. The gal who shares your bed but won't hold your hand in public is not your lover. It's sex. Not love. Period.

The Buddy avoids PDAs, never calls to thank you for a nice time, always goes dutch (or expects you to pay), and calls you up to hang out at the last minute rather than well in advance. Which means he or she is not *planning* to spend time with you. You are, my friend, are an afterthought. Second best. A consolation prize.

You know you're in a real relationship when there is at least *some* romance involved. Some public pecks, flowers or a gift on Valentine's Day, a sweet note left on your pillow. Heck, even if your mate isn't in to romance, at least you get dinner and a movie! Buddies don't do dates. They hang. It's casual. Spontaneous. *Friendly.* If your honey is really in to you, then you also get to meet Mom and Dad, go to parties as a couple, plan weekend getaways, and use words like "we" and "us" in everyday conversation. Do you have any of that?

Ultimately, it comes down to whether you're being loved *that way* or not. If you hear, "Love ya," instead of "I love you," that's a pretty good sign you've fallen for a Buddy. It's a cop out. And it's not romantic. But then, you're not lovers anyway, right?

The Myth of Commitment Phobia

So you think sweetie pie is afraid of commitment, and once he grows up and gets over it, or heals those broken wounds, he'll come around and profess his undying love. Okay. Let's discuss.

It could be that your gal is entrenched in some heavy-duty commitment phobia, and so treats you like a pal rather than her intended. But it's more likely that she just doesn't love you. Hard words to swallow, I know, but the truth is the one you pine for could find the love of her life tomorrow, and then watch how fast she runs to the altar.

Fear of commitment is a myth that people (that's you) tell themselves in order to explain why the one they love won't commit, plan, share, and generally treat them the way they want to be treated. In reality, when we find "the one," we have no qualms about signing up for a lifetime.

Take a friend of a friend of mine, whom I'll call "Susan." Susan spent two years of her life loving a man – we'll call him "Dick" – who seemed to be her ideal match. They both loved NPR and Walt Whitman, belonged to grassroots organizing organizations, and enjoyed ethnic food and music. They were two high-I.Q. individuals with identical values, compatible aspirations, and a rockin' sex life. Still, Dick never really committed to Susan. Oh sure, they spent a lot of time together, and he wasn't seeing anyone else, but Dick put up a wall that never came down. He avoided the subject of long-term plans and insisted he would not settle down until the next decade.

Ever patient and hopeful, Susan stuck it out with Dick. Eventually, they had a fight about his unloving ways, she wised up and left him once and for all. Fast-forward just six months. Susan receives an email from Dick, announcing his marriage to someone else. Someone he had known for just two months! So much for the pathologically single man Susan had waited so patiently for! Needless to say, she was crushed. In fact, I'm not sure if she's completely over it to this day.

Don't think for a minute that your guy or gal will one day be ready to go steady. If sweetie pie thought you were all that and then some, you wouldn't be reading this chapter. You'd be checking to make sure your *fiancé* wasn't some other kind of kook.

Why Do Buddies Do It?

I think by now you have a pretty good idea why your lover treats you the way he or she does. As the writers of *Sex in the City* proclaimed on the show and in the now-famous book and film, he's just not that in to you. Worse than that, she probably wasn't in to you from the beginning. At least not in *that way*.

But let's get beyond the obvious, shall we, and discuss why the Buddy keeps this charade up for so long. My friends, there are cowards among us. Losers that can't muster up enough courage to give it to you straight. Opportunists who don't want to lose their fuck buddy, personal ATM machine, or errand boy or girl, so they dangle hope in front of you like scraps to a dog.

The object of your affection *knows* how you feel. It's written all over your face. The right thing to do is tell you that you can never be more than friends – with benefits – but the Buddy won't do that. It's not that Buddy can't. Buddy won't. You're too valuable: Too willing, too patient, too available, and way too easy.

When you bring up your relationship, he won't look you in the eye. When you ask her to spend the night, she hems and haws about a 6:00 a.m. breakfast meeting or a sunrise dental appointment. When you try to make plans, he tells you he'll get back to you. But you also get a wink, a smile, or a playful pat. Just enough to tide you over until the next booty call.

The King and Queen of Denial (or Why YOU Do It)

Everyone loves a good mystery, and so the fact that your guy or gal is cryptic with his or her feelings adds to the allure. Agonizing over every conversation, every email, and every glance is exquisite torture. Right up there with the wonderful unknown is the fantasy finale. The moment when your lover finally reveals he is totally gone on you. You play it over and over in your mind, imagining what he'll say, how he'll say it, and the earth shattering sex you'll have to seal the deal. Your life starts to look and feel like a drugstore romance novel.

Meanwhile, the Buddy goes on with her life as if you are okay with the status quo (even though she knows you most definitely are not okay with it). Why should she let on that she knows? You never mentioned how you really feel. And why didn't you do that? Because you *know*. You know that when you finally reveal what you want, you'll learn the truth about how she really feels.

You're in denial, Honey. You're hanging on for the happy ending that at least some part of you knows will never come. This kook isn't going to run through the streets of New York on New Year's Eve in a rush to tell you he's madly in love with you, like Billy Crystal in *When Harry Met Sally*. You're not going to star in your own version of *Some Kind of Wonderful*, where in the last two minutes of the film, Eric Stoltz realizes he's really in love with his best friend and chases after her with diamond earrings in hand. It's real life, not *reel* life, and you're not going to get a revelatory moment out of this kook.

So step out of denial. I promise you'll be okay. In fact, you'll be better than okay. You'll be free to find true love. That's a whole lot better than solving this mystery.

How to Spot the Buddy

In order to spot the Buddy, you'll have to be honest with yourself. You'll have to look at your "relationship" without embellishing the facts. If you can't do it on your own, ask your most trusted friend to help you out. If your friend is a little on the brash or sassy side, all the better. To spot the Buddy, evaluate the following four phases of your "relationship" (notice how I keep putting the word in quotes? Hmmm...):

- **The Hookup**

Think back to when you first started up with your guy or gal. Did he ask you out on a date? Did she express interest in dating you? Did you slow dance, hold hands under the table, or make eyes at each other all night? If your "relationship" began with an actual date and then was followed by a series of more actual dates, you're probably not dating a Buddy.

If, on the other hand, your "relationship" began while you were just hanging out, you might be involved with a Buddy. If you never got dressed up for a date, never received a formal invitation to go out, and never heard your guy or gal refer to you as his or her "date," it's likely that you've fallen for a Buddy.

- **The Habit**

After the first whirlwind months of interesting dates and new experiences, most relationships eventually slide into habit. You can tell a lot about your "relationship" from its habits. For example, do you spend every Saturday afternoon at his mother's house? Does she expect you to come with her to her monthly gathering of college alumni? Do you take turns planning weekend getaways every quarter? Does she keep an overnight bag at your place? Does he have the Sunday paper delivered to your house since he'll be there anyway?

These are all signs of a real relationship, one in which you know your partner's friends and family, make plans, respond to expectations, and get comfortable with the commingling of your stuff. If any of this sounds familiar, you're probably not dating a Buddy.

In what way do you hang out with your guy or gal? Do you see each other only late at night after his 11:00 p.m. booty calls? Does she always seem to have plans after you take her shopping? Do you suggest most – or all – of the activities? Does he leave unexpectedly in the middle of a "date?" Does she come over to your place only when she's hungry, tired, or bored? If it seems like you are the Plan B, than there's a good chance you're involved with a Buddy.

- **The Milestones**

If you've been in a "relationship" for a while now, you've probably hit some milestones. While not everyone gets in to the little anniversaries, it is customary to at least acknowledge them. One month since your first kiss, three months since you started dating, that sort of thing. Some will give cards, flowers, or gifts. Others will just mention it in passing. But again, the acknowledgment is there, and it speaks volumes. It shows that your guy or gal really is dating you and cares about you enough to celebrate that fact.

Likewise, if your sweetheart remembers to give you something on a holiday or your birthday, it's a good sign that he or she is the real deal. But if you have yet to receive anything from your honey, not even a word about a special day, it's a sign that he or she is a kook who sees you only as a friend and convenient sex partner.

- **The Future**

This one's easy. Do you talk about the future together? A future with both of you in it, still together, perhaps even settled down? Does your gal expect you to come home with her for the holidays? Does your guy want you to decide where the two of you will vacation next summer? Do you both share simple fantasies with each other about where you might be in a year, or five, or ten?

If your guy or gal brings up the future and responds well when you do the same, it's likely you can cross the Buddy off of your kook list. But if your guy or gal can't even handle making plans for next week, you're in for a world of hurt. A Buddy has invaded your heart.

What if I'm Not Sure?

If you're still holding out hope that your guy or gal isn't a Buddy, it's time to take things to another level. The surest way to find out how your love muffin feels about you is to administer the test. Start with the first tip and work your way down. The beauty of all of these tips is they help you to look out for number one – that's you – in the process.

- **Set New Rules**

It's hard to change the rules of any relationship midstream. But if you want to smoke this kook out and take care of you, it's a must. Let your guy or gal know that you expect to go on dates, that you want to be introduced to the family and friends, and that you would like some acknowledgment that you are actually *in* a romantic relationship. If sweetie is into you, sweetie will rise to the occasion. If sweetie is a Buddy, sweetie will squirm.

- **Have "The Talk"**

If your guy or gal manages to wriggle out of the rule-setting discussion, it's time for the big guns. You need to have "the talk." Explain that you need to get clarity about the relationship. You want to know where you stand and where things are going. Gather your courage and let the chips fall where they may. The non-kook will realize it's time to get serious, and the Buddy will run for the hills.

- **Shop for New Baskets**

You've been waiting a long time for this kook to come around. Time to take your eggs out of one basket and spread 'em around. I'm not suggesting you get all slutty, but do start going out on real dates with other people, people who have a bona fide, even documented, interest in you. People with potential. Imagine that.

This step can be done if the other two don't work, but do realize you're taking a risk. If your guy or gal really is in to you, it might jeopardize your relationship. Or it could just cause your sweetie to wake up and smell the break up. A little competition never hurt anybody. Just don't do anything you wouldn't want your partner to do.

As I've said many times before, life is not the movies. If you're involved with a Buddy, you're not going to "get the girl" or "end up with the guy in the end." This kook isn't going to wake up one day and realize you're the one he's been looking for. If you were truly soul mates, she would have recognized you right off. It's chemistry, people. You either have it or you don't. And though your Buddy may eventually profess his or her love to someone, it's not going to be you.

The Clinger

Brent said Jenny couldn't go an hour without seeing, texting, or talking to him.

Nobody likes a clingy _____. Fill in the blank. Whether it's your boyfriend, girlfriend, husband, wife, or one-night-stand, nobody likes a Clinger. In fact, we have elaborate dating "rules" set up to remind us not to be "too clingy" or "too needy." When we meet a hot guy, we play hard to get. After a date with a dream girl, we wait four days before calling so that we don't appear too eager. The Clinger observes none of these unwritten "rules." The Clinger may not even know they exist.

I certainly do not advocate adhering to these parameters, and many relationships tank because people worry too much about showing how much they like this guy or that girl. Only you know what works for you and what doesn't, what constitutes moving too fast, and what just "feels wrong" in a relationship. Past this threshold is the point at which most Clingers get dumped.

So why do we even need a chapter about Clingers? After all, they're easy to spot. She's the gal who expects you to spend every waking moment with her just because you fooled around a little. He's the guy who calls you nine times to confirm your date on Friday. But this is what I like to call the "First Date Clinger," a person who may or may not be a kook. We've all dated people like this, and it often turns out that this otherwise perfectly normal person is either a) lacking in social skills and needs a little training, or b) hasn't dated that much or just re-entered the dating world after a long relationship, or c) is just totally gone on you and has completely lost his or her mind (in a good way).

But while this type of Clinger is a dead giveaway when you're first dating, spotting the kooky version can be a real challenge. Not all Clingers show their true colors right up front. Some wait until your good and gone on them to reveal their clinging ways, and by then it would take a lifetime supply of Static Guard to keep the Clinger away.

We dump the Clingers because they are annoying and make us feel uncomfortable. Clinginess is an instant turnoff. But in the context of a committed relationship, the Clinger may actually be dangerous. Possessiveness, the trademark trait of all Clingers, is really a method to control the one you "love," and is a harbinger of all things yucky – even deadly. Look up common warning signs of partner abuse, and you will find early possessiveness and "clinginess" at the top of the list.

So while you think you may know this kook pretty well and have already kicked a few to the curb, please take some time to read this chapter. Spotting a Clinger could save your Saturday night, but it could also save your life.

Muffin Is Just Really Into Me

Nope, Muffin isn't. Muffin is really in to the *idea* of you. It's not you; it's an illusion. AND Muffin is terrified that your relationship is only temporary. That's the fear part. So, illusion plus fear = Clinger x 10.

While you may be flattered by all of the attention heaped on you by the Clinger, don't fool yourself into thinking that your lover just has it real bad for you. If that were the case, she or she wouldn't be a kook. The difference between someone who is merely caught up in all of your splendor and someone who is pathologically possessive is that the former is having an authentic experience while the latter is lost in fear and illusion.

We all become irrational, babbling idiots when we fall madly in love with someone. We trip over our words and our feet. We stare at the telephone, willing it to ring, and check our email endlessly for cyber love notes. This kind of passionate, all-consuming love is real, and it happens, but even when we're wrapped up in the madness of it all, most of us maintain at least some semblance of healthy boundaries.

For example, you may feel a powerful urge to drive by his house every hour on the hour, but somehow you know it crosses a line. When you feel inspired to devote yourself to the woman you just met, some part of you knows it's too soon to share that information. Besides, it's fun to reveal these little secrets to your partner ten years down the road. Remembering how you used to be love-silly for your husband or wife is enough to reignite any waning flame.

Even though we may experience a rush of emotion when we meet "the one," most of us – the non-kooks – still manage to keep it together and follow traditional relationship protocol. Except for the Clinger. This kook has no idea that taking things at a natural pace and giving you space actually preserves the relationship. The Clinger has no concept of withholding declarations of love until the appropriate time or waiting until the "mood is right" to move the relationship forward.

So when you think this kook is "just really into you," remember how you act when *you're* really into someone. Would you even THINK of doing what your guy or gal is doing? I'm guessing...no.

Honey Bunch Is Just a Little Jealous

A girl loves it when two guys fight over her. It's an aphrodisiac. When a guy has three girls on a string, he feels powerful and potent. So when the Clinger starts with the jealousy act, we don't exactly think of it as a bad thing. It feels good to have someone love you so much that he or she doesn't want anyone else to look at you sideways. But this sort of behavior is fun only for so long. Soon enough it becomes annoying. Doesn't she trust you? (Nope.) Can't you even say, "Hello" to that handsome stranger? (Nope.) Do you have to get rid of all of your male friends? (Yup.)

Extreme jealous behavior is a sure sign of kookiness, but it's also an important warning sign of abuse. Anyone who can't handle it if you talk to, smile at, or spend any amount of time with someone who could be interested in you is messed up. Period. Jealousy can become an obsession, which never has a happy ending. How many wife-ran-over-husband-six-times stories do you need me to offer up as proof? Just pick up a magazine or watch cable TV for thirty minutes and you'll get your fill.

We always think it won't be us. We always think our story is different. It's not. The only difference between your story and that Lifetime movie of the week is the really bad stuff hasn't happened to you. Yet.

What's a good barometer for too much jealousy? When you start to modify your behavior to prevent your sweetie from getting angry. When you cancel activities with friends, keep to yourself, change the way you dress, come home at a specific time ordered by your partner, refuse invitations to dance with friends or strangers, and generally turn yourself into a shadow of your former self. Got it?

Clinger or Stalker?

Stalkers come in all shapes and sizes, but they all have one thing in common: they all believe you are destined to be together. It's a romantic notion, but a stalker can come to this conclusion having never even met you! And if you're not in to your stalker, his or her delusions are more like *Nightmare on Elm Street* than *Secret Admirer*.

Stalking is very real, and it happens more than you may realize. According to the Stalking Resource Center, a division of the National Center for Victims of Crime, one in twelve women and one in forty-five men will be stalked in their lifetime. And don't start giving strangers the evil eye. Statistics show that 77% of female victims and 64% of male victims know their stalker, and an intimate partner is the stalker for 59% of female victims and 30% of male victims. But the really scary statistic is that if your stalker is a current or former partner, the stalking often results in a physical assault.

Clinging is a controlling behavior, a possessive action that could be a warning sign of the stalking to come. In fact, some would argue that your sweetie's *current* behavior borders on stalking; again, it's not because he or she is really into you. Don't confuse possession with love. It's a dangerous game with no winners.

So is your sweetie a Clinger or a stalker? Could be your sweetie is one thing today and another tomorrow. If you're even the slightest bit concerned, contact the National Center for Victims of Crime, or your local Domestic Abuse Hotline, or your local law enforcement precinct. Just don't go it alone.

Why Do Clingers Do It?

The reasons why Clingers cling are many; what is behind your guy's or gal's bizarre and annoying behavior is a mystery you will have to solve on your own. It's complicated, and you may never figure it out. But basically speaking, all clinging behavior stems from fear. From the slightly needy bedfellow to the Stage Five Clinger from *Wedding Crashers*, all Clingers are plagued with insecurity that causes them to act like desperate spinsters on a last-ditch-effort date.

Insecurity is at the root of many psychological problems and challenging personality traits, so it's no surprise that this feeling is a major player in the Clinger's life. Your mate clings to you because he requires constant approval and reassurance due to the loss of a parent. Perhaps she needs control in order to feel important and worthy. Or maybe your honey clings because of a deep pathology that will eventually lead to an abusive relationship. No matter what the level of clinginess, this kook is feeling pretty insecure.

A word to the wise: Don't start stroking that insecurity itch. Filling the well of self-doubt is an impossible task; you'll soon spend all of your time trying to reassure your darling that he or she is your one and only. Your partner may never feel sure of you, or your relationship, so don't make it your business to try. It's easy to get sucked into the self-worth dance with someone you love, but unless you want to be part of a codependent duo, let your guy or gal work on this one from the inside out.

The Center of the Universe (or Why YOU Do It)

Admit it. It feels good to be adored. You like feeling wanted. Needed. Special. The Clinger lays it on thick and it feels good to hear how amazing you are. How life would be impossible or meaningless without you. How you were meant to be together. Since we took our first steps away from our parents, we have yearned to return to the time we were the center of the universe. The Clinger takes you there by showering you with attention. Hard to say, "No" to that, isn't it?

For some people, the reason we allow ourselves to hook up with a Clinger is more complicated. As I mentioned earlier, clingers often morph into stalkers and abusers, and those type of people prey upon the insecure, the damaged, and the lonely. For someone with poor self-worth, the possessive tendencies of a lover may seem like love. But as the relationship progresses, any confidence this person gained from the attention is shattered by violence and manipulation.

Understanding what attracts you to Clingers is key. Do you need to feel controlled in order to feel loved? Are you looking for an all-consuming love? Are you searching for a partner who will give you all of the attention you never received? Get real about why you wanted this kook in the first place. And work on building your self-confidence. When you feel strong and secure, dangerous Clingers will just walk on by.

How to Spot the Clinger

As I said earlier, the early Clinger is easy to spot. In fact, you are not likely to enter into a relationship with obvious Clingers because, quite frankly, they're freaky. They reveal too much about themselves right up front, make themselves too available, contact you constantly, and follow you around like a shadow. But what about those shifty Clingers who win your heart before revealing their real identity? Here are a few signs you may have a Clinger in dreamboat clothing:

- **Overtly Independent**

Smart Clingers know the drill. Reveal too much about their true nature, and you're out the door before the second date. So these kooks adopt an "independent girl" or "no commitments guy" personae to call you off the scent. They make sure you know that they are their own people , with goals, friends, responsibilities, and, probably, other love interests. He's the guy who just wants to keep it casual but still wants to see you all of the time. She's the gal who plays coy about her other lovers but always seems to be at your place.

Make no mistake, the Clinger disguised as a disinterested free-spirit is just lying in wait, watching your every move in search of signs that you are good and hooked. It won't be long before the annoying behavior shows up, and possibly worse. Just remember, actions speak louder than words.

- **Slowly Isolates**

Like any good crazy, the Clinger will slowly attempt to isolate you from your friends and family and everything you love to do solo. It's a gradual process, so you may not notice it at first. Wouldn't it be nice if you didn't have to go to church, so the two of you could sleep in on Sundays and eat breakfast in bed? I'd really like to take that dance class with you, but the only day available is the same day you meet up with the girls. I don't think your family likes me, and I don't feel comfortable going over to your folks' house anymore.

You love this person, so you cancel this and reschedule that. Soon your life is one long date with your sweetie, interrupted only by work and errands. If your Clinger is pathologically clingy, then you probably can't do anything on your own, and you may end up mired in an abusive relationship.

- **Changes Rules Overnight**

During the early stages of any relationship, flaws are covered up and quirks are hidden. We're courting, and we need to put our best selves forward, which means something different to each of us. This is also the time that we are more apt to compromise, to express understanding, and to forgive.

But the Clinger isn't just holding back a few annoying habits. The Clinger's waiting for a shift in the relationship, such as moving in together or getting engaged, to change the rules completely. One minute your gal thinks your boys-only weekends are cute, and the next minute she threatens to leave you if you go. Before your wedding your guy never worried about your male buddies, but as soon as you said, "I do" he barred you from seeing them.

Getting serious with a secret Clinger can leave you feeling blindsided. By the time you figure out there's something kooky about your beloved, you've signed on the dotted line. And because your mate's got leverage, he or she isn't afraid to let it all hang out. And you never saw it coming. Or did you?

What if I'm Not Sure?

Dating a Clinger is frustrating because you *want* to spend time with your sweetie, but you also need space to breathe your own air, spend time with friends and loved ones, and pursue your own interests. If you want to try and work it out, take this advice to heart:

- **Set Clear Boundaries**

Clear and healthy boundaries are a key component of satisfying relationships, even if you're already hitched. When someone steps over the line – any line – it makes you nervous. Yet in the thralls of new love we often let our sweeties cross that line and smile while they're doing it. We worry about hurt feelings and potential breakups. It's time to get those boundaries back in place.

Make a list of what you want your partner to stop doing AND start doing. For example, perhaps you would like your guy to stop calling you at work and start calling before he comes over. Or maybe you want your gal to stop asking questions about old flames and start leaving you to your own devices on game night. If your list is really long, consider couples therapy as the best venue to reveal the list. If it's short, ask your guy or gal to come up with a similar list, and then trade.

- **Slow it Down**

Hot and heavy hookups are one thing, but escorting you to every family function is something else entirely. If you're worried that your lover may be a Clinger, slow things down a bit. You don't have to have "the talk" about how you need more space, blah, blah, blah. But you do need to make a conscious effort to avoid major relationship milestones and keep things light. It takes two to tie that knot, remember?

- **Take a Time Out**

Of course, you may need to bypass boundary reorientation and braking maneuvers and go straight for an old fashioned time out. You can clear your head, get some perspective, and sort out how you really feel about this potential kook. Best yet, you'll probably get definitive proof of your honey's Clinger status.

Clingers hate time outs, as do most kooks (except Solo Artists), so yours will probably reveal his or her kookiness during your break. He'll drive by your house to see if you're there, call up your friends to ask if you're seeing anyone else, call you and text you and email you, even though you don't want that. She might even get angry and threaten you with a final breakup, or vandalism, or even bodily harm. Nothing smokes out a Clinger like a time out!

If your lover can't handle the new ground rules you set forth, it could be a sign of dark days to come. Only you know if his or her reaction doesn't feel right. If he really wants happily ever after, he'll accept your terms and try to lay off the clinging. If she's a primo kook with a dictator complex, she'll put up a fight. Express your concerns to your friends and family, and get a second opinion. Your peeps will help you sort it all out, so clue them in and then decide.

Remember, if you feel even the slightest bit uncomfortable, it's too much. Your friends might think it's cute that your guy or gal hangs on you like white on rice, but if you don't like it, it's not. You've got to nip this one in the bud, before the Clinger takes root in your heart.

The Control Freak

Tracey said Billy was so controlling that he checked her email, recent calls, AND her Facebook page twice a day.

Ever heard of an accident waiting to happen? Well, if you're in a relationship with a Control Freak, you're in a tragedy waiting to happen. There's a whole heap of psycho driving this kook, and the longer you stick around, the more you put yourself at risk with a capital R. The MOST dangerous of all of the kooks, the Control Freak is an abuser in disguise, and no amount of unconditional love is going to change that sad-but-true fact.

She's the gal who drives by your house at all hours, just to make sure you're not out with someone else. He's the guy who likes to grill you, hoping to catch you in a lie. Control Freaks are the people who feel threatened when you make a move without them, even if it's just to sign up for a Saturday morning pottery class. Every decision, from wardrobe to wedding plans, MUST be cleared through this kook. So much for maintaining your own identity. Did your really make it through your adolescence just to toss that hard-won personality in the trash?

Some people mistake Control Freaks for another type of kook. The Clinger, The Narcissist, the Guru and even the Neatnik all have controlling qualities, which may lead to a misdiagnosis. It's easier to put your money on kooks who aren't as scary as the Control Freak, people you think you can handle, but don't lie to yourself for too long. You have way too much to lose.

Sure, you may be right about your guy or gal. Maybe she is *just* a Guru trying to mold you according to her "more perfect" vision. But she may also be a Control Freak biding her time until she can reveal her true, monstrous colors. You could be spot on about your guy's Neatnik ways, but he might show up at your door as a Control Freak at any moment. Will it be too late?

Are you scared yet? Scared enough to honestly take a look at this partner of yours? Because the signs are there, I promise you. They always are. Ask those who have been victims of domestic violence. They'll give you a list of things that should have tipped them off, things they brushed aside or chose to ignore completely. Signs that, had they heeded them, may have saved them from a heart in pieces and a life in ruins.

So take a long, deep breath and dive into this chapter. I said it about the Clinger and it's true for this one, too: If you're dating a Control Freak, your ability to spot *this* kook could save your life.

Money Master

Let me. No really, *let me*. It starts with little things that seem chivalrous and benign. He pays for dinner. She picks up the bar tab. Nothing weird there. But then he chooses the restaurant, determines the date and time, and orders your food for you. She arranges the meeting place, limits your drinks, and tells you when it's time to leave. Every. Single. Time.

Control Freaks *have* to be in charge of the money because it gives them ultimate power over what you do, when you do it, and with whom you do it. If you're still living independent lives with separate bank accounts, these kooks can still get control by offering to pay for everything. You think it's cute, but all of that generosity is just a tool to show you who's boss. Once you do hook up permanent-like, Control Freaks take over completely.

Not having their own money or *access to their own money* is often the reason why people stay in abusive relationships. Control Freaks know you're not going anywhere if you can't get the cash, so they set out to become money masters right off the bat. One day you have a life, a job, and a decent savings account; the next day you're totally dependent on your partner. If you even *think* your guy or gal *might* be a Control Freak, hang on to your dollars and never tell your sweetie how much you have or where it is. You never know when you might need a little road trip cash.

(You do know you CAN get out, right? If you feel stuck in a bad relationship because your partner controls the money, find an alternative. It may not be fun, and it may not be pretty, but at least you'll be safe. Call a friend, a family member, or a local shelter for help. Don't let money be the reason you stay with *anyone*, kook or not.)

Spy in the House of Love

Control Freaks routinely spy on their partners because they assume they're lying through their teeth. These kooks don't trust anyone, and they're bound and determined to prove just how naughty their partners really are. Even if you're friggin' Julie Andrews, the Control Freak will find a way to catch you "being bad." A complex set of rules and crazy logic will be thrust upon you so that you're doomed to fail every test this kook sets up. You'll have to modify your behavior to the extreme to keep this kook happy, so much so you'll end up acting like you wandered off from a compound in Texas.

Before you end up a prisoner in your own house, watch out for the early signs. He hacks into your email account. She creates an alter ego online in order to catch you cyber flirting. He checks your phone records and calls all of the mysterious phone numbers. She calls the receptionist at your job to ask if you're really working late. He drives by, she shows up unannounced. They keep tabs on your old lovers, read your credit card statements, and "bump into you" in the oddest places.

Don't think for a minute that this type of behavior is a sign that your guy or gal cares about you. It's controlling, sick behavior, and it's never about love. And it's also not about a bad break-up in the past or a wounded childhood; that stuff can be worked out in therapy, thank you very much. What's really behind all of this spying is a cruel desire to prove what a loser you are, to see you fail. How romantic.

Drill Sergeant

As soon as Control Freaks get you to commit on any level, their inner drill sergeant comes out of the closet. These kooks want what they want when they want it, and you damn well better do it the right way or there *will* be hell to pay. This bullying behavior won't show up until you're good and gone on this kook, so don't think your guy or gal is off the hook just because you haven't met the taskmaster…yet.

When you go away for the weekend, your guy feels compelled to show you how to properly pump gas, read a map, and choose car-appropriate snack items. When you get ready for an interview, your gal tells you what to where, drills you on how to answer questions, and shows no confidence in your ability to do well. Control Freaks inspect your clean floors for dirt, take boxes of your stuff to the Goodwill, and hover over you at the gym to make sure you're working out "correctly." Again, this level of Control Freak may not appear immediately. (If it does, and you stay in it, march right to a cognitive behavioral therapist and make an appointment. You need help, Honey.)

Then again, you may have seen shadows of the drill sergeant. Have you received detailed instructions about how to do something basic, something you know how to do? Have you been asked to change the way you clean, shop for groceries, make a bed? What about the way you drive, dress, or even the way you carry a conversation?

It starts with the jibes. First you get to hear how silly you are. Then you get to hear how stupid you are. Eventually, you will be told you don't know how to do anything right and will be schooled in the correct way to do everything. Cutting asides and little comments about your laugh, your "lack of knowledge" on a certain subject, your choices - they are all signs that a Control Freak is vying for your heart...and your soul.

Why Do Control Freaks Do It?

Self-loathing and insecurity drives this kook, and it's buried down deep where even you can't find it. Maybe your guy grew up with an overbearing parent who never spared the rod. Perhaps your gal was belittled and criticized as a child for every little thing. However it happened, Control Freaks learn pretty early on that they aren't worth much. Left locked away to fester and grow, this pain morphs into some serious rage. And that rage is behind every controlling act this kook dishes out.

Control Freaks are broken. Someone somewhere taught them the only way to feel good was to be in complete control of their nearest and dearest. If they were broken over and over again, they were also taught that the only way to feel *really* good was to put the fear of God into their nearest and dearest. Enter the abuser.

Batterers are made, not born. Look to your sweetie's family for clues. Is it common knowledge that his mom got knocked around a lot? Did her mom make her feel like she never measured up? How do they handle conflict? Are you allowed to disagree with his parents? Are there oodles of rules in her parents' house?

Even if your sweetie never raises a hand to harm you, that doesn't mean that your life won't be miserable. Control Freaks need help to deal with the past that made them who they are. Your gal may tell you she just needs your love and support, but she needs more than you can give. Your guy may want you to believe that he just needs some time to figure it all out, but time cannot heal his wounds. Control Freaks need therapy. Lots and lots of therapy.

If you are dating a Control Freak and fear for your safety even just a tiny bit, contact your local Domestic Abuse Hotline. At the very least, you can learn about the options available to you in your community. You may even learn about an organization that could help your sweetie. And don't forget to program the number into your phone under one of your friends' names. You never know when you may need it.

Top 10 Hottest Beasts and Bitches (or Why YOU Do It)

Strong men and women are hot, plain, and simple. Most of us prefer to date people who know what they want and aren't afraid to take it. We may say we would like to settle down with Jennifer Aniston, but we'd like to *get it on* with Angelina Jolie. And James Dean was WAY hotter than Jimmy Stewart, even though Jimmy was much better husband material. We, and by "we" I do mean me and you, like bad boys and girls who could potentially get us into trouble, steal our hearts, and give us the best sex of our lives.

Control Freaks are strong in their convictions and confident in their choices. There's something dangerous about them, and that's exciting. For now. They like to be in charge, and following their lead is a nice switch for a change. At first. They're powerful and demanding, and that's kind of hot in more ways than one. Until it's not.

Look, there's a big difference between a badass and a bad match. If you're attracted to the dark side, why not just go for the tough ones that take it out on society or make art? Find a sweet kindergarten teacher with a secret penchant for tattoos. Hook up with a rabble-rouser fighting for fair wages and health insurance. Date someone who gets your juices flowing but still wants you to be you. You can have a healthy relationship with a badass, as long as that badass has a sound mind and a good heart.

On the other hand, you may be attracted to Control Freaks because you equate love with being overpowered and overruled. For whatever reason (only you would know), you don't trust someone who trusts you, and you don't know how to love someone who loves you well. Some part of you gets off on being bullied, and before you tell me how wrong I am, remember, no one ever does anything without getting something out of it.

Now I'm not saying you want to be verbally bruised or physically battered. I'm not saying you want to spend the rest of your life in a rule-infested prison. What I am saying is there is something about this kook that turns you on, and it may be worth figuring out what flips your switch. Otherwise, you'll end up right back where you started – dating a Control Freak and wondering why.

How to Spot the Control Freak

Spotting this kook is pretty easy; just count how many times you get to make a decision, win an argument, and generally feel awesome about yourself. Control Freaks are in charge, always right, and prone to making you feel pretty shitty. So if you have an equal partnership, if your opinions are respected, and you feel pretty damn special around your sweetie, it's a safe bet he or she is NOT a Control Freak.

But keep reading, just in case. Here are a few more ways to spot this kook:

- **Just the Two of Us**

The "just the two of us" trick - it's as old as time. Control Freaks (and SO many other kooks) isolate you from the people who love you most in order to make you feel, well, isolated. And to keep those pesky BFFs out of your business. After all, if you can't spot the kook, your friends sure can. In a heartbeat.

Control Freaks don't trust your friends and family, and they don't trust you when you hang out with your friends and family. Heck, they don't even trust the mail carrier. Why did you say, "Thank you," *that way*? Do you have something going on with the meat counter guy? Your receptionist has the hots for you. Where are you going? I don't like it when you go places without me. Who will be there? I don't think they like me. I don't feel comfortable around them. We have so much more fun together, *just the two of us.*

If your guy wants you all to himself all of the time, take notice. If your gal would rather you stay home alone than go out with your friends, pay attention. Isolation is a sure sign that you're dating a kook, and that kook could very well be a Control Freak.

- **You're Wearing THAT?**

If you're still allowed to roam free, the Control Freak will have something to say about your appearance. Control Freaks see you as an extension of themselves, and so the way you look is a reflection of them. You've got to dress appropriately, get the right haircut, and generally adhere to their image guidelines. How you look in public is also a trust issue for these kooks, who worry that you're dressing provocatively or pumping up your muscles in order to attract a new lover.

Controlling your appearance stamps out any hope of individuality. How we present ourselves to the outside world is our way of telling people who we are. Our wardrobe is our uniform, giving clues to our values, interests, and even aspirations. When Control Freaks pick at what you're wearing or try to completely alter your look, it's an attempt to remove any trace of you from your appearance. They may say it's for your own good or to help you get where you want to go, but it's not. If your guy or gal is trying to outfit your life you may be dating a Control Freak.

- **Why Do You Have to Push My Buttons?**

Does it seem like your sweetie is always mad at you? Do you feel like you just can't get it right? Do you walk on eggshells around your gal, afraid to make a wrong move? Do you try to keep your mouth shut so your guy won't freak? Do you routinely change your behavior with your guy or gal to keep the peace?

Control Freaks can't stand it when you disagree. Or do something they asked you not to do. Or say something they don't want you to bring up. Underneath that controlled façade is a heaping pile of rage that could be set off by the tiniest thing. There is no logic to it, either. Control Freaks are unpredictable when it comes to their temper. As soon as you figure out how to keep them happy, they freak out about something else and turn into one big ball of anger. This is about the time you get to hear, "You should know better," and, "Why did you have to push my buttons?" No matter what your guy or gal is raging about, there is one thing you'll hear for sure. It's. All. Your. Fault.

If your guy or gal has a short fuse and blames you for setting it off, get out and get out fast. Don't even bother finishing this chapter.

What if I'm Not Sure?

I'm pretty sure you're sure but still need to be convinced. Okay, look. This kook is REALLY kooky. This kook is scary. This kook is not going to change. So if you think your guy or gal is kinda sorta a Control Freak, and you plan on trying to find out or work it out, do me a favor and complete ALL of the following tasks:

- **Stash Away Some Money**

Don't let lack of money keep you in a bad relationship. Right now, today, set up a secret bank account so you can start stashing away money. If you don't have money of your own, ask your friends and family to donate to your cause. Deposit whatever you can whenever you can because the more you have the easier it will be to get away fast and move on with your life.

- **Get a Safe Place**

Determine the safest place you could run to should you ever have to get away from your partner. Even if you're just dating this kook, you may need a night or two away if things get ugly. Find a place that will be a safe haven for you, a place where your guy or gal would never find you. Just knowing you have a place to go will make it loads easier to walk out the door.

- **Hatch an Escape Plan**

Money and a safe place are only two components of an effective escape plan. You need to get organized. (Just in case, of course.) Make copies of all of your important papers – your will, bank info, IDs, birth certificate, etc. – and store them with a trusted friend or family member. Think about what you might need if you had to stay away from home for a period of time. What about a different cell phone? A secret credit card?

Plan your escape. You may never have to execute the plan, but knowing you have one in place will help you feel empowered.

When someone truly loves you, he or she wants you to be happy, to be free, to be you. True love does not come with conditions, rules, or requirements. Love should free you, not imprison you. Love should lift you up, not beat you down. Love should feel awesome, not scary.

If you're in love with a Control Freak, you have to get out. There is no other option. No matter what you change about yourself, no matter how hard you try, you're never going to be able to make this relationship work. The controlling behavior is only going to get worse. You will lose more and more of yourself with each passing day until you are a shell of person, living in fear of the love that seemed so right for you once upon a time.

Are you content to sit in the back seat for the rest of your life? Yeah. I didn't think so. Control Freaks are SO not worth it. You, on the other hand, are TOTALLY worth it. Really. You *are*.

The Cyber Citizen

Ellen said Michael was so hooked on the Internet that he cancelled a hiking trip when he found out they would be out of signal range.

Cyber Citizens seem like harmless kooks. Heck, at least they're home, right? While it's true that these geeks are tamer than most kooks, a Cyber Citizen can cause just as much strife and sorrow in your relationship as the other kooks. Internet porn and online gambling are just two of the pastimes that could cause serious problems for your bank account, your sex life, and, most of all, your heart.

Even if your sweetie is honest and true, Sweetie could still be a Cyber Citizen; this kook is not always a schemer or cheater. Very often there's something *else* going on with the Cyber Citizen, an underlying problem with intimacy and commitment or a penchant for obsessive behavior. A more serious mental health issue could also be at hand, such as an anxiety or anti-social disorder, masked by what seems to be a "simple" Internet addiction.

Of course, acting like a Cyber Citizen could just be a front. Maybe your guy is leading a double life or having an affair, keeping in touch with his other squeeze(s) via IM and a secret Facebook page dedicated to *their love*. Perhaps your gal is all about identity theft and is busy spending other people's money in the great big mall that is the World Wide Web.

Whatever the reason behind the kooky behavior, you need to get to the bottom of it. Unfortunately, it can be hard to spot a Cyber Citizen at first because our society is so technology-obsessed. (I confess, I am a techaholic.) It's not unusual to see two people texting on their date or a couple working on matching laptops. But you will figure it out eventually, probably about the time you realize your guy or gal would rather break up with you than give up the WiFi.

The (New) Couch Potato

You may think your honey is just über cool, a hipster with some serious Internet savvy, but it could be that he or she is just a modern-day couch potato. Don't be dazzled by his 10,000 plus "friends" or the legions of followers that comment on her self-indulgent blog. Being popular online is easier than making friends in real life.

To have an active social life in "real time" would mean actually getting his or her butt off the couch and *seeing real people*, maybe even, I don't know, walking somewhere. Making real-life connections requires being present in people's lives, sharing actual experiences and showing that you care. It could be that your guy or gal is just lazy, but it could also be that your geeky couch potato is actually afraid of human interaction.

Couch potatoes, whether big readers, TV addicts, or Cyber Citizens, are hiding from something. Everyone needs an occasional night (or weekend) of brain drain and Ben & Jerry's, but to spend every free moment glued to the couch is a sure sign that your sweetie is avoiding something. The computer is just an excuse, a hobby that legitimizes his or her fear of real life.

Fantasy Freak

Beyond the couch potato Cyber Citizen is the fantasy freak, the guy or gal who REALLY can't deal with real life. The Internet offers endless opportunities for fantasy interactions, from online porn to interactive video games that simulate your "other life." Your kook could be indulging in a little secret identity action, creating an online personae – or several. It may be a Pandora's box, but doesn't that seem like something you should know about your one and only?

We've all heard stories of people posing as someone else online, in chat rooms, on forums, and on blogs. This scenario is so common it's part of pop culture, a plot point in film, television, and books. Sometimes it's predatory, sometimes it's dishonest, but it can also be just plain fantasy fun. Even if your guy or gal is the latter, the fantasy is hard to give up.

You have to ask yourself, why does my sweetheart need the fantasy? What's missing from his or her life that compels them to create an alter ego and keep that myth going with nameless, faceless strangers? Good question, right? You may want to phrase it a little more delicately, but it is important for you to find out why your guy or gal spends so much time pretending to be someone else.

Thrill Seekers & Sex Junkies

So what else could your sweetie be doing online? Hmm. Let me think. Oh! I got it! Gambling and porn. How silly of me to forget the top two Internet time wasters. Not your honey pie? Are you *sure*? Online gambling and porn sites are humungous industries raking in billions from average Joes and Janes all over the world. We're talking instant gratification and serious thrills, all just a click away. How could you NOT consider this scenario as a possible reason for the Cyber Citizen's behavior?

Part of the allure of virtual casinos and online pornography is the fact that you can do it privately in your own home. You may think she's just hanging on Facebook while you both watch TV, but she may have lost $10,000 in the time it takes Jon Stewart to deliver the news. You don't question the time he spends working on his "small business start-up" late at night; meanwhile, he's on a first-name basis with every pay-per-view hottie in cyberland.

It's not too hard to figure out if your partner is frequenting these websites. Just check his or her browsing history to find out. If the cache is cleared, check out the email. If you see loads of random email messages from suspicious sites hell-bent on titillation, it means your dream-come-true probably joined at least one of these sites. And don't believe it when he or she tells you it's all spam. Some of it, maybe. But not ALL of it. If you can't get your hands on the laptop, just check out the finances. Look for strange charges on bank statements and credit card statements and you'll figure it out in short order.

Why Do Cyber Citizens Do It?

There are so many reasons why a person may develop into a Cyber Citizen I'd have trouble listing them in one book, let alone one chapter. We've gone over a few and they do all have one thing in common: The need to escape from reality. Shopping, gaming, gambling, posing, chatting, or sexing it up with total strangers take you out of your daily existence swiftly, providing instant relief to what ails you.

So could your Cyber Citizen be an "Internet addict?" The jury's still out on whether or not compulsive Internet use is an actual disorder. In fact, the term Internet Addiction Disorder (IAD) was actually a spoof propagated by an M.D. Still, some mental health experts do feel it is a real disorder, especially when Internet usage interferes with normal function in daily life. However, those who disagree point out that it's just like any disassociative behavior in that it is a symptom of a larger psychological problem.

One exception is online gambling, which is really just gambling in a different venue; the fact that the bets are placed online is not the issue. Gambling addictions are a different animal altogether. If your partner is in deep with gambling, he or she is not a kook. Your partner needs help.

The National Council on Problem Gambling (NCPG) explains "problem" or "pathological" gambling as, "A progressive addiction characterized by increasing preoccupation with gambling, a need to bet more money more frequently, restlessness or irritability when attempting to stop, 'chasing' losses, and loss of control manifested by continuation of the gambling behavior in spite of mounting, serious, negative consequences." That's some serious stuff there, and if you really care about your sweetie, you'll get him or her some help.

Geeks Are Cool (Or Why YOU Do It)

At first glance, Cyber Citizens are cool cats. They've got pimped-out computer setups that can do everything, and they make your own laptop work so well, it practically purrs. She's beyond Internet savvy and knows the best blogs and the hippest sites; his fingers fly across the keyboard, opening and closing windows at lightning speed. If you were being honest, you'd admit it kind of turns you on.

Since the Cyber Citizens can be hard to spot, I'm guessing you probably didn't know about their kooky habits. At the very least, you didn't grasp the depth and breadth of the problem. But you *did* hook up with someone who is preoccupied with the unseen, favors fantasy over reality, and can only achieve intimacy with a computer screen. And even if you didn't know that person was an honest-to-blog kook, you certainly did catch a whiff of somethin'. What does that say about you? Hmm...maybe that you're not ready for a "real" relationship, either? If you're not sure, ask your therapist. Or your best friend. And as a last resort, your mother.

BUT, if you absolutely knew the truth of your sweetie's kookiness, if you willingly signed up to date Cyber Citizen, then maybe you're also a supreme geek with your own Internet addiction. Addicts hooking up with other addicts – how unusual! (Not!) Two geeks in love is poetry, two kooks in love is a movie of the week – and *not* the one with the happy ending.

On the other hand, maybe you just figured, at least my honey's not out carousing. At least he or she is at home, snuggled up to you and the router, instead of drinking, drugging, or fooling around. So...how's that logic workin' out for ya? Still happy with that decision? Yup. I didn't think so.

How to Spot the Cyber Citizen

You'll never spot the Cyber Citizen out in plain sight. Internet junkies need long, private surfing sessions that just aren't practical in public, even at the hippest coffee shop. Pay attention to this kook's habits at home and at work, and you'll start to see a pattern of Internet use abuse. Here are a few more telltale signs that you've fallen for a Cyber Citizen:

- **Constant Companion**

If she takes her laptop to bed, knows all of the wireless hot spots within a 90-mile radius, and can't make it through dinner without checking her PDA, your gal is a Cyber Citizen. If your guy has two backup computers, stops what he's doing every time his mailbox beeps, and fires up his browser before he takes a pee in the morning, he's a bona fide cyber kook.

A non-kook has the ability to ignore the instant messenger and go days without checking his or her favorite blogs. A non-kook goes on wireless-free vacations, closes the laptop in order to look you in the eye, and actually knows how to use a phone book. Can you say the same about your one true love?

- **The Latest and Greatest**

The Cyber Citizen spends a lot of money on technology. A *lot*. The next time you're at your sweetie's place, take a peek around. Are there lots of empty equipment boxes lying around or in the recycle bin? Is there more than one computer in the house? Is there a wireless router sitting next to the bed? If there's more technology than food, a Cyber Citizen lives there.

Don't forget the portable gadgets. Look in the car, at the office, and in the briefcase or purse. And how much time does your sweetie spend shopping for new stuff? Can he or she pass up an electronics store without going in? Are the Apple Store geniuses on speed dial? Add it all up. If it all seems too much, it probably is.

- **First Things First**

When your sweetie puts his or her online adventures before you, consider it a red flag. If he or she prefers to surf the net rather than have sex, you've got a red flag so bright, it's on fire! We all have reasons for avoiding our main squeeze, and there could be a whole host of issues behind not wanting to get frisky. But if it's clear that you're on hold until your sweetie's urge to surf is satisfied, I'm here to tell you there is a Cyber Citizen in your bed.

What if I'm Not Sure?

We all go through obsessive phases wherein we indulge in something a little too much, and your guy or gal may just need a little reminder that there is life on this planet. Follow one or all of the following suggestions, and you'll learn the truth in short order. No real Cyber Citizen will be able to make it without totally freaking out!

- **Engage in Minor, Temporary Sabotage**

What's wrong with a little sabotage in the name of love? As long as it won't hurt your sweetie's business, finances, or creative endeavors, I say go for it. Figure out how you can temporarily cut off all access to the World Wide Web and also how you can get your guy or gal back online, if necessary. The Cyber Citizen will totally crumble and go in search of an Internet connection or a computer. A reasonable person will deal with it and find something – or someone – else to do until the problem is solved or the computer miraculously appears.

- **Request a Hiatus**

One way to find out if you're dating a Cyber Citizen is to suggest a break from the Internet and see what happens. Plan a trip to a remote area, turn off the wireless, whatever it takes to get your darling to log off and focus on you and your relationship. The kook won't have it or will agree and then engage in illicit surfing, so at least you'll know what you're dealing with. Remember, the hiatus applies to you, too!

- **Set up Technology-Free Zones**

Establish areas or times when technology or online time is not allowed. Make your bedroom a laptop-free zone, limit surfing to the work hours, or the morning, or whatever works for you. If you find your guy or gal Googling in the closet, you've got a problem. On the other hand, if he or she is a Cyber Citizen waiting to happen, setting up ground rules for Internet usage will help both of you manage this problem and keep it from getting out of hand.

Googling binges, constant texting, checking email every two minutes – these are also the pastimes of the Cyber Citizen. Laptops as appendages, multiple email accounts, state-of-the-art surge protectors, these are the tools of the Cyber Citizen. He or she may not be scheming or dreaming, but too much is too much, no matter what the obsession turns out to be.

What you need is a partner who is engaged with you, not zoning out on bandwith. The Cyber Citizen is tuning out on everything, shifting his or her attention to the real world just long enough to do the bare minimum, such as keep a job, eat food, and get laid. It won't be long before you want to toss that laptop in the river and run over the PDA with your car. After all, it's tough to be jilted for another human, but to be routinely passed over for a computer, well that just sucks. Aren't you worth more than that?

The Doom and Gloom

Patrick said Diane's dark side was so dark that she couldn't even be happy when he proposed.

Do you want the truth? Are you sure? Because this kook's story is a sad, sad tale – and it doesn't have a happy ending. The Doom and Glooms are kooks who live in a fantasy world, one where nothing ever turns out the way they want it to, the rug gets pulled out from under them when they least expect it, and they have to pay for the good news with bad news. I use the word "fantasy" because we all know that life isn't really like that, even if it feels that way from time to time. But this kook really believes the world is one big accident waiting to happen.

The Doom and Glooms may have perfectly justifiable reasons for their malaise, but that doesn't mean they plan to change. They may say they want to change, but these kooks are addicted to the dark side. She's the gal who has ideas and plans but can't seem to get started because she's convinced she'll fail. He's the guy who spends most of his time complaining about how the world treats him. The Doom and Glooms are people who can't enjoy their accomplishments because no matter how great they are, they will never be enough.

Consummate worriers, these kooks will never be happy. They can't. They're addicted to doom, gloom, and everything in between. And they're good at it. Even when they're up, they're anticipating – even plotting – the way back down. Which means you're going down, too, because these kooks always need a blues buddy. Try as you may, this one will never see the light. Are you ready to spend your Saturday, your summer, or the rest of your life tied down to the prince(ss) of darkness?

But Adryenn, My Dumpling Wasn't Like This When We Met!

You aren't likely to meet Doom and Glooms in a dark period. You're going to meet them when they're up, or at least up enough to date. The Doom and Glooms are hard to spot in the beginning because the fact that they're dating at all is a sign that they're feelin' groovy. To be receptive to love – or even friendship – requires at least a semblance of hope, an openness to new possibilities, and a willingness to try something new. If your guy or gal were down in the dumps at the first chance meeting, he or she wouldn't have been receptive to you at all, and it's not likely that you would have felt inspired to swap phone numbers, either.

Though your sweetie may have been full of smiles and laughter when you first hooked up, it was only temporary. In fact, it was only ever *meant* to be temporary. The key to the Doom and Gloom's kookiness is that he or she believes true happiness can never be attained. Even when high on a peak, he or she is just resting on the way back down to the valley.

Whether it's weeks or even months into the relationship, when the kook finally does show up it's like invasion of the body snatchers. Your once carefree sweetie has morphed into the poster child for negativity. Everything sucks, all is lost, and he or she knew it would eventually happen anyway. A dark cloud hangs over everything, and you start to wonder if it was something you did or didn't do, said or didn't say. It's not you. It's the kook.

Note: Kooks aside, some of the signs I described above could actually be symptoms of bi-polar disorder, a manic-depressive disease that is serious but can be treated. If you think your guy or gal may be suffering from this or some other mental illness, it's time to seek professional help. Start by contacting a trusted family member who may be able to help you get your sweetie to see a family doctor or therapist.

Do You Want the Bad News, or the Really Bad News?

For the Doom and Glooms, there are only two kinds of news: Bad and worse. Not only do they see the glass as half-empty, they think it is only moments before the glass is tipped over, and the water is lost forever. You'll notice it when your honey expects the worst every time you "want to talk," or when he or she opens the mail with trepidation or gets anxious about a meeting with the boss. But all of that is nothing compared to the bad news this kook imposes on him or herself.

The "Doom" part of this kook is all about the anticipation of disaster. You may hear about some of your sweetie's fears, but most of them are kept hidden safely inside his or her psyche. You see, the Doom and Gloom runs a constant tape of negativity – a.k.a. doom – inside his or her head at all times. It won't work out between the two of you. You'll leave eventually. He or she is not good enough. Yadda, yadda, yadda.

We all have at least some self-confidence issues and lack of self-esteem in at least one area, if even for a short period of time. There's a whole industry built up around eliminating negative thought patterns. Take the recent phenomenon, *The Secret*. The movie and companion products made millions because so many of us want to rid ourselves of limiting beliefs and thought patterns, thereby manifesting our true desires.

But the difference between the Doom and Gloom and the rest of us is that this kook can't see that his or her thoughts *are* negative. This kook sees negative thoughts as facts, and all of the bad things – from red lights to skin cancer – are just evidence of being right all along.

It Hurts So Good

People don't do anything if they're not getting something out of it. I know it sounds odd, even creepy, but the Doom and Gloom gets off on the pain. The "Gloom" part of this kook is the state of being that follows the Doom, a feeling of despondency that pervades his or her entire life and rubs off on yours. If you're in deep with this kook, then his or her despair is more than a little annoying, it's gut wrenching.

Human beings are creatures of comfort. We do what we know to do, over and over again, even if it's not good for us. We get involved with the same train wreck of a person every chance we get, we return to old, destructive habits even though we know they're wrong, and we stay in our own little bubbles, rarely venturing out of our very cozy box.

When I say "we," I mean everyone. Even you. That's what the self-help industry is all about. Getting out of our comfort zones, especially those that are unhealthy, and living an authentic life. We need books, classes, workshops, tapes, and good counsel from friends and professionals to finally leave our wives, take up mountain climbing, quit our jobs, ask for our jobs back, return to college, change religions, and lose weight.

So it's no surprise that a kooky version of you and me, namely the Doom and Gloom, would have a tough time getting out of that bad news rut. Something about the melancholy is familiar and reassuring, because he or she knows how to do it. Besides, when down in the dumps, your sweetie gets tons of attention, doesn't have to take risks, gets to talk about his or her feelings, and generally is the center of attention for the duration. That's the part that "hurts so good."

Until your darling realizes what he or she gains (and stands to lose) by getting off this cycle of doom and gloom, he or she will always come back to the mythical land of losers. Darling has been to the Despair Diner so often that Darling's a regular. They know your guy or gal there. They save your darling a seat. And he or she gets free apple pie. Beats reality. You know the one where people try to better themselves and choose optimism over, say, Armageddon?

Why Do Doom and Glooms Do It?

There is a very fine line between a Doom and Gloom kook and someone suffering from clinical depression or some other psychological challenge. Some people are depressed, and you can spot them by their will to change. It may be a small will, and it may take years to heal, but unlike the Doom and Gloom, non-kooks are not using their gloomy disposition for personal gain.

Very often, the Doom and Gloom is also another variety of kook, like the Narcissist, the Lost, or the Baby. Non-kooks may also exhibit some of these tendencies, but they are usually symptoms of depression. As I stated in the previous section, the kooks get pleasure from the roller coaster ride of emotions. The non-kooks desperately want to get off the ride. While both types may be stuck in a comfort zone of pain, the non-kooks know they have to learn how to create new comfort zones and are hopefully working on doing just that.

If you suspect that your guy or gal is depressed, by all means, stop reading this book and get your sweetie some help. Sweetie may not want it, but if you love your him or her, you'll do your best to get Sweetie the help the desperately and obviously needed.

Depression, gone untreated, can wreak havoc on your sweetie's life and may end in suicide. In fact, according to the Kristin Brooks Hope Center (www.hopeline.com), untreated depression is the number one cause of suicide. The Center, which was founded by Reese Butler, whose wife, Kristin Brooks, committed suicide in 1998, launched the first national suicide hotline, the National Hopeline Network. When you call the Hopeline (1-800-SUICIDE), you are automatically connected to the crisis center closest to you, allowing your loved one – and you – to get help locally, and fast.

So is your guy or gal depressed or kooky? Only a medical professional can diagnose someone with depression, but there are a few signs that may help you identify the disease. According to the National Institute of Mental Health (www.nimh.nih.gov), the following symptoms are signs of depression:

- Feelings of emptiness, hopelessness, and pessimism.
- Feelings of guilt and helplessness.

- Insomnia or over-sleeping.
- Lack of energy.
- Lack of self-worth and ability to make decisions.
- Loss of appetite and/or weight loss.
- Loss of interest in pleasurable activities, such as hobbies, social gatherings, and sex.
- Memory loss and difficulty concentrating.
- Overeating and weight gain.
- Persistent anxious or sad mood.
- Persistent physical symptoms such as headaches, digestive disorders, and chronic pain that do not respond to treatment.
- Restlessness and irritability.
- Suicidal thoughts and suicide attempts.

If your partner is clinically depressed, hang in there. The disease can be treated, and your sweetie can go on to live a healthy, happy life. But if your guy or gal is a Doom and Gloom kook, he or she's got problems that not only may never go away, they also insult those who truly suffer from the devastating disease that is depression. So, not only is this kook super kooky, he or she's also a jerk.

My Love Will Set You Free (or Why YOU Do It)

It feels good to make someone's day. It feels even better to help people find their way, see the light, and make a new start. In fact, it feels so good that some people seek out the Losts and Babies of the world just so they can get a hefty dose of that "helping high." For those of you who find yourselves attracted to the Doom and Glooms, the urge to fix these kooks may be more powerful than the love you feel – or *think* you feel. You've got a savior complex. And you've got it bad.

Only you know why you might be drawn into the web the Doom and Gloom spins. For some reason, you just can't get enough of trying to help these kooks back onto the Yellow Brick Road. I'll bet you can just hear the Oscar acceptance speech now: "I want to thank my sweetheart. If it weren't for so-and-so (that's you), I never would have made it this far. So-and-so (you again), I owe you everything. This award – and my life – is yours."

Listen up and listen good. You're not man or woman enough to pull this off. Your guy or gal is a *dedicated* pessimist. He or she made this doom and gloom stuff an art form; it's his or her raison d'être (that's "reason for being," for those of you who took Spanish instead of French). If you absolutely must offer your wisdom and influence to your bed buddy in order to feel in love, then go for the Lost kook. At least you'll have more fun.

How to Spot the Doom and Gloom

If you've read the symptoms for depression, and your guy or gal doesn't fit the bill, it's time to play "spot the kook." Again, you may not see these signs when you're first hanging out, but if you look hard enough, you can spot at least some of the following traits:

- **Drama Junkie**

Perpetually self-involved, this kook is so prone to drama, he or she puts daytime TV to shame. The Doom and Gloom milks every mishap and misunderstanding for all its worth and then some. This "woe is me" personae takes every little bump in the road as evidence that he or she was right all along. This person's cursed. Condemned to a life of disappointment. Doomed.

This drama junkie seeks out the traumas and tragedies like a cokehead in search of a fix. She's the gal who gets involved with every dilemma and argument in her family, even if the family is thousands of miles away. He's the guy who, in long-winded emails and phone calls, regales you with stories of his endless hardships. If there's a problem, you're going to hear about it. And hear about it. And hear about it. Because what good is the drama if you can't rehash it for hours on end? And if you have a problem of your own you need to discuss, don't expect to get what you need. This kook will make your problem his or her own by the end of the conversation. Oh, the drama!

- **Excessive Worrier**

Worrying is a hobby of the Doom and Gloom, and it's one of the few traits you may be able to spot early on. Why? Because worrying is very hard to keep in check. Even if this kook is trying to hide pessimistic preferences, he or she will find it very hard to stop worrying completely. Instead, your dearest may indulge in some benign worries. Will Brad Pitt stay with Angelina Jolie? Will the Dodgers go all the way this year? Does this skirt make me look fat?

Or you may get to see some serious worrying that requires your immediate reassurance. What if my house starts on fire? What if my doctor finds a lump in my breast?

What if I don't get that promotion? What if you want to see other people? If you hear a lot of "what ifs" early on, it's a sign that your sweetie may be a Doom and Gloom. At the very least, he or she needs to get some help for what may very well be an anxiety disorder. Hot, right?

- **Never Satisfied**

No matter how much the Doom and Gloom accomplishes, it's never enough. Never satisfied, your guy or gal can't stop to appreciate the wins. He or she may say, "Thank you," but that's just politeness. There's no attitude of gratitude for this kook, and contentment is just an abstract concept – or a pipe dream.

You'll notice this behavior in the backhanded comments your sweetie makes about his or her accomplishments. He only got the job because no one else showed up for the interview. She'll probably screw up the opportunity somehow. You only chose your guy or gal by default. Dissatisfaction with circumstances is usually what motivates people to make positive changes in their life. But for this kook, it's not a jumping off place. It's a way of living.

What if I'm Not Sure?

I understand why you're not sure about this one. If you're really in love, the last thing you want to believe is that your sweetheart is beyond help or, worse, doesn't want help at all. You want to hold out hope that tomorrow will be better. But if your guy or gal is a Doom and Gloom kook, there's very little you can do to change his or her deep-seated beliefs. If you plan on staying with this one or want to see if you can live with a professional pessimist, then take the following advice to heart:

- **Encourage**

You may be right. Your sweetie could be in need of encouragement, a personal cheering section to kick those gloomy thoughts to the curb once and for all. It never hurts to be encouraging to your partner. And who knows, maybe he or she will see the light this time. Just remember to heap your praise, and then let it go. This relationship is a perfect candidate for co-dependency, so pat your sweetie on the back and then change the subject. You can't force a flower to bloom by pulling off its petals.

- **Disengage**

This kook will suck you in and drag you down. If you're not sure if your muffin is a bona fide Doom and Gloom or if you have a pretty good idea he or she is one and you plan on staying with Muffin anyway, the first order of business is to disengage from the drama. You can listen, you can be supportive, but you need to do your best to disinvest your emotions in his or her problems.

Of course when you do, the kook's true colors will appear. Your darling will feel betrayed and wonder if you plan on leaving him or her for someone less troubled. (Umm...can I vote "Yes?")

Disengaging protects your own psyche – and heart – and the consequences may be enough to make you realize you are dating a kook. Or, if Muffin's really just in need of a minor personality adjustment, he or she will realize you were right to practice a little self-preservation and will (hopefully) take steps to get out of the Doom and Gloom cycle. Hey, one can dream, right?

- **Live Your Life**

This bit of advice is key, but it is also tough to follow. If your sweetie is a Doom and Gloom, or is clinically depressed, or just has a problem with self-esteem, you need to remember to take care of yourself first. If you're planning to help nurture your partner away from the dark side, you'll need all the strength you can get. Ditto if you plan to leave your partner instead.

So get out and do what you used to like to do. Laugh. Play. Have fun. Follow your dreams, revel in your accomplishments, and enjoy your friends. Just because your sweetie has chosen a life of unending disappointment does not mean that you cannot live your own life to the fullest – and love every minute of it.

Time to face facts. This kook is never going to be one of the shiny, happy people. This person can't do shiny and most certainly cannot do happy. Your guy or gal is mired in the muck. You are not. Remember that. Although your sweetie's problems may take up most of the space in your relationship, you do actually have your own life with your own interests and your own issues. You probably even enjoyed it, once upon a time.

Whether you decide to make up or break up, remember, you used to have chaos-free days and drama-free nights. You used to date people who had goals and followed through. You used to wake up without dread, fearing what your partner may be dealing with that day. Even if you stay, you need to get back some of what you left behind. So if he or she needs help, offer to assist your sweetie in getting it. (If you think your partner's depressed, *make sure* he or she gets it.) But don't forget to take care of you. Misery loves company, and that's all this kook has to offer.

The Grifter

Michael said that by the time he got a clue, June had drained his savings and maxed out his credit cards.

Ah, the Grifter. That master of the deception that captures your heart – and your wallet. How we do love to immortalize this kook. Time and time again, the thief lover is portrayed in film, on television, in music, and in novels. It's fascinating to watch the Grifter pull the wool over someone's eyes as we "tsk tsk" the victim and say out loud, "I would never fall for that." But you could. And if the conditions were right, you probably would.

The Grifter is the kook who claims to worship the very ground you walk on and then absconds with your money, property, and other valuables (ummm…what's the going rate for your heart?). She's the gal who coos at the sound of your name yet secretly has mastered how to forge your signature. He's the guy who seems mesmerized by your beauty but expects you to buy him a sports car to keep him happy. The Grifter is the person who, when it comes to relationships, has one thought on the brain: "What (and how much) can I get out of this person?" That means you. What can the Grifter get out of *you*?

Grifters come in all shapes and sizes, but they are chameleons who know how to change their appearance in order to a) be your fantasy lover and b) disguise themselves from former admirers (should they wander out of the homeless shelter and spot them escorting you to lunch). This kook can alter his or her speech, personality, likes and dislikes until he or she fits your idea of a perfect match. You see, the Grifter has to catch you and catch you good, winning you over so completely that you would do almost anything for your new love. The Grifter wants your implicit trust, and once that, phase one, is accomplished, he or she can move on to phase two: Bleeding you dry.

There are dangerous Grifters and Grifters who wouldn't harm a fly. Grifters can be jerks who bully their way into your heart, and they can be angels who swoop down and carry your heart off on a fluffy cloud. Whatever works for you, the Grifter will do. Until.

Until the Grifter gets what he or she came for and leaves you high and dry crying in your soup. Which you can't pay for anymore. Okay, maybe half a cup, tap water and some saltine crackers. But NO tip.

By The Time You Read This, It's Already Too Late

Spotting a Grifter before he or she makes off with the loot is tricky. If you suspect your sweetie is not all he or she seems and so are reading this chapter, I'm sorry to tell you it's probably too late. Rarely do Grifters slip up enough to get your shackles up, and by the time they do, the die is cast.

Grifters are the fastest kooks in the land, working systematically to win your heart and pad their own pockets. To complicate matters, this kook may have a long-term payoff in mind, such as property (my honey would never kick me out; we're in love!), division of assets (we don't need a prenup; we're in love!), or inheritance (so what if Honey's forty years younger than me; we're in love!). But even if the Grifter is into the long con, it's still too late. Once your heart is tied up in knots, there's very little hope you'll come out unscathed.

Excuse Me; Are You Using that Identity?

A broken heart and an empty bank account are nothing compared to the loss of self. I don't just mean the fact that after the breakup you feel like a shadow of your former self, I am referring to identity theft. Grifters are experts at obtaining enough personal information about you to assume your identity for personal gain. They may use your name and social security number to open credit cards, sign a lease, buy a car, or even obtain a driver's license and passport.

Horror stories about identity theft are rampant in this country. If your identity is stolen, get ready for the battle of a lifetime. It can take years, even decades, to clear your own name from the Grifter's transgressions. Identity theft is hard to prove and could ultimately land YOU in jail, paying for a crime that your former flame committed. And you thought the fact that he or she ran up a charge at Bloomingdales was a big deal!

Beyond outright identity theft, the Grifter may simply use your existing credit cards to make purchases, or use your name to gain access to exclusive clubs, or make verbal agreements. This kook is savvy and knows how to time the steal by taking a little bit here and a little bit there so that you either don't notice or brush it off as a bank error or miscommunication between the two of you. But again, you probably won't catch it in time. You're too busy to reconcile your bank account or glance at your credit cards bills. You're in love!

My Baby Doll Would NEVER Do That to Me!

I'm always amazed at how many people tell me they never saw it coming. Really? You had absolutely no idea? When I probe a little further, I usually hear something like, "Well, there was that one time I found my ATM card in her purse, but she took mine by mistake." Yeah, right. Here's another good one: "I did think it was strange that he bought the car using my Amex, but then he reminded me we had talked about it the week before." Okay, then.

Why are we so willing to trust a virtual stranger with our private affairs and personal documents? Because love makes us do foolish things. That's why you need to spot this kook right up front, before your heart is hooked. It's awfully hard to say, "No" to the person giving you the best sex of your life, isn't it? Never mind the fact that this person seems to really "get you" like no one has before. He or she believes in you. When you're with your sweetie, you feel you can move mountains. You never knew it could be like this. Yup. You're screwed.

The Grifter is such a skilled actor that there is very little chance you will see through his or her declarations of love and devotion. The best you can hope for is an early spot, so you can escape this kook before he or she even has a chance to say, "Hello."

Why Do Grifters Do It?

The simple answer is the Grifter wants money. Your money. Valuables. Property. Stocks. Whatever the Grifter can get. But the reason behind that could be as different as night and day. Circumstance can make a "regular" guy into a master of manipulation; the desire for financial security can lead a "God-fearing" woman down the gold-digging path.

Does it really matter why the Grifter chooses the life of a con artist, rather than a real artist, or banker, doctor, or organic farmer? Not really. Once this kook gets a taste of getting something for nothing and experiences the incredible adrenalin rush from committing fraud, the Grifter is lost forever.

When a Grifter crosses over from petty acts of fraud to diabolical deceit, he or she becomes a sociopath. This could happen in childhood (yes, it's true) or later in life. Like the Narcissist with whom the sociopath shares many qualities, there is a continuum, a scale by which to measure the level of pathology. The guy who dates you for two weeks and steals just enough cash to pay his rent is a bit lower on the sociopath scale. The gal who hires a hit man to take you out to collect your fat insurance payout is WAY on the other side of the continuum. But both are sociopaths just the same. Sociopaths can be violent, and many serial killers are sociopaths, so don't think for a minute that your very own kook is just a tame puppy having a run of bad luck. Your puppy might just be wiling to do ANYTHING to get what he or she wants. ANYTHING.

The sociopath does not feel compassion or remorse. Again, like the Narcissist, a sociopath is grandiose, complicated, and NEVER considerate of the well being of another living thing. Hot and bothered? I certainly hope not. If this section doesn't dampen that flame, nothin' will!

The Grifter, whether a sociopath or a run-of-the-mill lazy opportunist, is a big time kook. If you've bumped up against a Grifter, you need to learn how to protect yourself. I recommend you visit the website of Donna Anderson, a former victim of a class-A con artist. Her site, www.LoveFraud.com, has helpful information and links to forums and other websites that will help shed light on this dangerous kook.

Too Good to Be True (or Why YOU Do It)

No one will (appear to) love you more intently, more passionately, than the Grifter. You want hot, earth shattering, can't-eat-can't-sleep kind of love? No problem. That's this kook's specialty. When he looks at you, his gaze seems to burn right through to your soul. When she smiles at you, your entire body turns to jelly.

Very quickly, the Grifter assumes his or her role in your life, the role you've been waiting for. The Grifter isn't just a really great date; the Grifter's *the one*. This kook isn't satisfied with being liked. This kook wants to be the only possible person who could make you happy. Otherwise, how would he or she be able to pull off such a major scam? Anything less than complete devotion, and you might keep your desk drawer locked and hide your car keys. If you don't love this kook completely without reservation, you might figure out he or she has only one thing on the brain: The big fleece.

My friend, if a Grifter has hoodwinked you, you are not to blame. This kook is hard to spot and easy to fall for. Your Grifter figured out what you needed, and gave it to you – in spades. Your Grifter became the person of your dreams. But don't forget, your Grifter wasn't that person until he or she discovered that's what *you* wanted.

However, I do wonder how badly you wanted it to be true. Did you fill in the blanks for your sweetie when things just didn't add up? Did you ignore that guardian angel on your shoulder, whispering in your ear? Did you brush off inappropriate behavior in order to keep the peace? Were you so desperate to keep the fantasy of the perfect mate that you threw caution to the wind and gave over everything that mattered to you?

The Grifter is *always* too good to be true. So if you find yourself saying, "I almost don't believe it! I'm so in love. This person is my dream come true!" to your best pals, remember the *first* part of that declaration. You almost don't believe it. Which means you don't believe it at all, you just want it to be true. Because you want the Grifter to be the real deal, you'll do almost anything – including hand over all your money, time, trust, and self-respect – to make it so.

How to Spot the Grifter

As I mentioned earlier, because the Grifter gives Oscar-worthy performances on a daily basis, spotting this kook is harder than finding that age-old needle in a haystack. Besides, you'll be too busy wallowing in his or her admiration and adoration to even *think* about the signs. When the Grifter finally has you where he or she wants you, expect the following signs to pop up pretty regularly:

- **You Pick up the Tab...A Lot**

While initially this kook is more than willing to spring for dinner or go dutch on the B&B, it won't be long before he or she stops paying for anything. Her big real estate deal is still in escrow, and she'll pay you back as soon as the ink dries on the contract. His ex-wife tied up all of his assets, would you mind floating him until his attorney can straighten it out?

If you're picking up the tab most – or all – of the time, I have no doubt you're dealing with a Grifter of some sort. Sure, we all have slow seasons and are strapped from time to time, but if we truly love the one we claim to love (that's you, Honey), the very last thing we would do is mooch off of our beloved. Absolutely, when two people marry or enter into a legally binding partnership, money is often shared. But not to the detriment of one partner or the family unit.

- **You Get to Save the Day...A Lot**

The hallmark move of the Grifter is an urgent crisis. Right up until this point, however, this kook probably went out of his or her way to take care of you. Then it happens. One day he shows up at your office looking glum with a story about his big deal that's about to fall through if he doesn't come up with $5,000 by the end of the day. Or she calls you to say goodbye because her former boyfriend got her fired, she now has to leave her apartment and move in with her folks. Cue trumpet-blaring hero music. Enter, you.

The Grifter tugs at your heartstrings and often makes you think you've come up with the brilliant solution to his or her problem all on your own. Wasn't it your idea to co-sign on a $40,000 loan for his new business? Didn't you offer to pay for her scouting trip to Hollywood? If your sweetheart has more financial crises than cash, you hooked a Grifter. Time to throw this one back!

- **You Defend Your Honey to Your Friends...A Lot**

Now that you've invested more than just time and love into your relationship, you're not about to let anyone get in the way of your (expensive) happiness. When your best friend takes you aside out of concern for your welfare, you find yourself telling tall tales – just like the Grifter – in order to get your friend off your case. You start leaving out details in your story and always sound hopeful, even when you're scared to death.

Do you find yourself putting on armor every time you meet your buds for drinks in order to protect yourself from inquiring minds? Do you catch yourself making up stories and explanations about your guy or gal at important social functions? If you are regularly defending your honey from the judgment of your loved ones, you might be involved with a Grifter.

- **You Hear Excuses...A Lot**

Excuses and lies. The Grifters are full of them. In fact, these kooks are so creative they could be a brilliant actors, politicians, or Wall Street executives. But no. Your Grifter camped out on your turf, handing you one load of crap after another and expecting you to swallow it with a smile. The Grifter always has a reasonable reason, a bona fide excuse for the lack of funds or the need for more funds. The Grifter is hard to argue with and soon has you believing that he or she either a) holds the world record as the unluckiest person in the world or b) is underappreciated, undervalued, and under-loved. Boo hoo.

If your darling frequently assails you with silly excuses and wild tales in order to appease your concern and worry, he or she could be a Grifter. At the very least, Darling's hiding something from you. Don't you want to find out what it is?

What if I'm Not Sure?

Unfortunately, all of this time you've spent waffling about – maybe my pumpkin is, maybe my pumpkin isn't – Pumpkin has probably cost you some hard earned cash. Grifters work fast, so even if you're not sure if your guy or gal is "on the grift," take steps NOW to protect your identity, your bank account, and your heart.

- **Change Everything**

Make a list of every password you have – online bank accounts, ATM card, even your Amazon.com password – and change all of them to something your lover would never guess. It's a good idea to change passwords regularly, anyway.

If you suspect your sweetie has been dipping into the cookie jar, switch banks and change all of your credit card numbers. It will take half a day to get all of this done, but it could save you a fortune.

- **Put Everything Under Lock & Key**

Go through your important papers – bank, credit card, and utility statements, blank checks and check stubs, quarterly reports from your financial advisor and investment portfolio, deeds, titles, birth certificate, social security card, etc. – and then file them in a fire-proof safe box. Keep the box at work or at your parent's house, away from prying eyes and nimble fingers. Or open a safe deposit box at a bank you normally do not patronize and store your documents there.

- **Investigate**

First, dig around your own finances to find out if your sweetie has overstepped any boundaries. Then, run a credit check on yourself from all three credit bureaus to see if he or she has been using your identity to open credit accounts. Make sure you sign up for credit monitoring as well.

It's inexpensive, and most companies will send you an email when changes post to your reports or when credit companies present inquiries.

Do some old-fashioned snooping and find out all that you can about your guy or gal. If you hit a roadblock, hire an investigator to do it for you. Well-informed is well-armed, and you can't afford to be ignorant. There's always a chance that your dumpling is on the up and up (though I doubt it), but if Dumpling is a Grifter, Dumpling may be wanted by the police (that I don't doubt), and you could be harboring a fugitive. It sounds a bit romantic, if you like that sort of flick, but as I say time and time again – life is not the movies!

The Grifter is no ordinary kook. The Grifter does more than break your heart. This kook ruins your life. Every move the Grifter makes, every vow the Grifter takes, is all designed to gain your trust – and your money. The mistake many victims make is looking for the heart in the kook. It seems impossible that your lover could say and do all of those things to you and with you and mean none of them. Well, my friend, stop searching, for the Grifter has no heart.

And unlike the Tin Man in the *Wizard of Oz*, he or she is not looking for one, either.

If there's even a remote chance that you're involved with a Grifter, and you still refuse to give up on him or her, may I suggest you start learning all the ways you can cook a box of rice? Because that's what you'll be eating for years to come. A box of rice. Maybe some almost-expired chuck roast and an onion or two. A cup of noodles. Processed cheese. Yum.

The Guru

Paige said she was so used to allowing Walter to fill in all the blanks that she forgot what it was like to make a decision.

The Guru can set your life on fire, turn it upside down and right side up again, and help you become the person you always dreamed you could be. The Guru's charming, charismatic, and has all the answers. The Guru will rock your world and make you feel alive in ways you never thought possible. But with all of this wonderment going on, it's pretty hard to see the kook behind the curtain. But kook the Guru most certainly is, and it's best you figure that out before you transform your life any further.

A true guru is someone who provides spiritual instruction, but the modern usage of the term has expanded to include any expert offering to share his or her wisdom with others. In the dating world, a Guru is a kook who imposes his or her wisdom on you to the exclusion of your own ideas and experiences.

She's the gal who introduces you as a member of the profession *she thinks* you should be in. He's the guy who asks you to prove your commitment to his way of thinking by abandoning your hobbies, friends, goals, and belief systems. Gurus are kooks that get off on guiding you toward excellence and revelation and get angry whenever you step outside their carefully constructed lines.

Dating a Guru is a heady experience, much like dating a rock star or televangelist. This kook can really work a room (or stadium), and the fact that he or she chose you over everyone else makes you feel super special. You feel like you're part of something important. The Guru has big ideas and strong convictions, and best of all, the Guru believes in you wholeheartedly.

Despite your fantasies, Svengali-like relationships rarely last. Human beings are made to evolve, and unless the Guru is willing to let you grow beyond the scope of his or her vision you will have to cut ties in order to thrive. That is, if you manage to stay in the Guru's good graces for long. The

Guru has an ego that requires constant stroking from new initiates, so it won't be long before you're passed over for the next impressionable cutie who crosses this kook's path.

The Meaning of Life for $200

When it comes down to it, we're all searching for the meaning of life. We want to feel connected to our higher purpose, to confidently walk toward our destiny on a well-lit path. Even if you're not consciously thinking about the big questions, you may be feeling that something is missing from your life. Most of us have something we'd like to change or better about ourselves – our bodies, our minds, the size of our bank account.

Enter the Guru, who is an innovator, a visionary, and a beacon in the night. This kook has been where you are now and has a foolproof plan for getting you out of your rut and into the light in no time. Not only do you get to date this wunderkind, you get to benefit from the Guru's wealth of experience as you work to craft the life he or she has imagined for you.

Some Gurus make a living off of their kookiness and could also be Grifters looking to charge you for every single revelation, every last manifestation. Even if your guy or gal is not the ringleader, you may drawn into a web of "free" sales seminars and pricey products that are required tools on your journey toward enlightenment or wealth through rental properties – whatever comes first.

At this point, you may be thinking your sweetie is off the hook just because he or she doesn't have a congregation or an online following. Wrong again. Not all Gurus monetize or "legitimize" their kookiness through entrepreneurship, religion, or both. Some of the most manipulative kooks are disguised as everyday folks with strong opinions and an eagerness to share their story with you.

The Guru wants to guide you, teach you, and show you the way. It could start as innocently as making suggestions about your clothing or the way you wear your hair. Soon you're reading his favorite authors, considering a career change, and consulting with him before you make move one. Eventually, you're seeing her therapist, changing your diet, and skipping out on family "things." Your friends suddenly seem hopelessly out of touch, and you feel drawn toward your sweetie's more enlightened friends. And you just don't understand how the rest of the world can be so clueless, amoral, lost, and confused. Right. *We're* the crazy ones.

While these examples may seem extreme, if you do plan on sticking it out with this kook, you'll have to modify your life to some extent. The Guru needs you to be the malleable student so that he or she can see some tangible, measurable evidence of his or her "profound" influence on your life.

So, what are you going to give up first?

Pet Project

Remember, the Guru gets off on your transformation, so expect to be shown off to all of his buddies, all of her closet pals. You're this kook's pet project, the proof that he or she can work magic and knows what's best for you – and everyone else. You might feel special on his arm until he tells the room what a dork you used to be. And while she may seem proud of all you've accomplished, it won't be long before your accomplishments or beliefs are dismissed with a patronizing pat on the head.

Worse, this kook may even try to take credit for your successes, even if all he or she did was provide the initial kick in the pants that started you on your quest. But then, where would you be without this kook? See, he or she will make you feel as though you were mere moments from absolute destruction, a heartbeat away from the homeless shelter, career suicide, a heart attack, or eternal damnation. But really, was your life all *that bad* before you met this kook? And be honest now, isn't there *some chance* that you could have made positive change on your own?

My Way or the Highway

Gurus have very little patience for disagreeable companions. In fact, anything less than hero worship is grounds for dismissal – yours, that is. If you're dating a Guru kook, say goodbye to your own opinions, thoughts, and feelings. And because this kook has shades of other kooks, such as the Control Freak and the Narcissist, you may also have to say goodbye to a few other little things, like your self-esteem, safety, and sanity.

When this know-it-all becomes part of your life, there's very little room for anything else. No dissenters allowed. So if your family and best buds aren't down with your new guy or gal, it won't be long before your Guru suggests – or demands – that you spend a little less time with them. Anyone who undermines the Guru's plan to completely take over, er, I mean *revitalize,* your life will be yesterday's news before you wake up and realize the truth: That this kook plans to completely take over your life. Oops. Did I say that already?

Why Do Gurus Do It?

As I stated before, the Guru thrives on influencing others. On paper it seems like an ego thing, which is annoying enough, but scratch the surface of this kook, and you'll find a grab bag of insecurities underneath. The Guru *needs* you to look up to him, to find her advice revelatory and inspired. The Guru may seem supremely confident, but really this kook needs reassurance that he or she has the right idea about things. And you, my friend, *are* that reassurance.

With you hanging on his every word, your guy feels like he has something important to say. The fact that you follow her lead like a guide dog in training makes your gal feel worthy of all that mooning and cooing. Painfully, *painfully* insecure, the Guru is in a constant search for external validation. Once the Guru finds "the way," this kook stops at nothing to confirm his or her decision was exactly right.

Some Guru's are really crafty, charismatic types who consciously manipulate you with one goal in mind: Control. They're power freaks, hell- bent on micromanaging your every move. Very often these Gurus are quite dangerous, using threats and violence to keep you in line once you realize they can't, in fact, pull a rabbit out of a hat. At the very least, this kook is not all he or she seems and, worse, probably isn't in love with you at all. How could love from this person even be possible since you are merely a reflection?

What My Lover Sees in Me (Or Why YOU Do It)

Most of us want to better ourselves; we all have something that we'd like to change, improve, or manifest. So we're all easy prey for the Guru, really. But if you're a little lost, confused, or are a tad lacking in self-worth, the Guru's going to nab you in seconds flat. Especially if the Guru's cute – and Gurus are *always* cute.

Low self-worth can easily lead people down a well-manicured path towards subjugation, and almost no one is immune to the Guru's charms. Intense and charismatic, it's hard to say, "No," to this kook, so don't kick yourself too hard for saying, "Yes." We all fall in love with how someone makes us *feel about ourselves*, and for those of us who have low-*ish* self-esteem, the fact that the Guru sees "so much potential" in us is too intoxicating to refuse. We want more. And more. And more. We want to live up to the vision our Guru sees for us because we never thought any aspect of that vision was possible.

It could also be that you've got a secret Daddy or Mommy complex - a need for someone to look up to, someone to obey, someone to set the rules and take care of you. You may need a teacher, someone to guide you through life, to help you weigh decisions and chart your course. You could also simply be star struck. It happens every day. I'm not talking in terms of celebrity; I'm referring to the people who just have "it." She owns the room. He's everyone's friend. She's going places, and you want to come along. He's at the top of his game, and you feel special just standing by his side.

Whatever your reason for loving this kook, it doesn't make you weird or crazy or stupid. It just means you want something more out of life, and you're looking for answers. You don't need me to tell you to look inside yourself first, right? I mean, you've pretty well got that figured out by now, don't you? Good.

How to Spot the Guru

Lucky for you, the Guru is easy to spot. Like any good mentor, Gurus pay attention to you and encourage you and provide you with answers to life's most-asked questions. Your guru will try to change you by "inspiring" you and "showing you the way," and never *once* will consider the possibility that he or she may have something to learn from you, too. That said, here are more ways you can spot this kook:

- **Arrogant, Much?**

Although at first it may seem like the Guru has self-confidence and strong convictions, it won't be long before this kook's true arrogant nature is revealed. He or she is frequently condescending and occasionally rude, especially after you've been together awhile. See, your guy thinks a lot of himself, and he expects everyone else to see the wonder that is him, too. And your gal knows she's an extraordinary human being, and so she believes she has earned a pass when it comes to good behavior. In other words, the rules of "polite society" do not apply to this kook.

- **All the Misguided Souls**

Ah, the little people. If only they had access to the Guru's wisdom. After all, everyone – yes, *everyone* – is so misguided, so ignorant; they're all savages, really. For the über evolved (or devout, or successful, you fill in the blank) Guru, there is no better subject than the clueless masses. How the Guru loves to talk about all of the lost souls, the hopeless minions. He or she may have an optimist's take on it, but even if your Guru's Florence friggin' Nightingale, he or she still thinks we're all in need of a serious life makeover.

- **I Come Bearing Gifts**

The Guru almost always comes bearing gifts. The tools of this kook's trade may be inspirational CDs, DVDs, or podcasts; they may be a "must-read" how-to book, a weight loss supplement, or a convention full of fellow believers. The upside is you get stuff, but the downside is you're supposed to think it's the most amazing, life-altering stuff ever known to humankind. And if your Guru has made a career out of sharing his or her wisdom with others, these gifts are merely to entice you to buy. Buy into the dream, the vision, the theories; buy into the program, the seminar, or the timeshare. Make no mistake, this kook's selling, and *you're* buying.

What if I'm Not Sure?

Yes, it is possible your guy or gal is not a Guru. It could be that your sweetie is just super excited about life and wants to share it with you. Maybe Sweetie does have some answers you've been looking for, and maybe he or she genuinely likes you just the way you are. Maybe. If you're not ready to give this one up, here are a few tips to help you deal:

- **Share and Share Alike**

Bottom line, is your sweetie willing to learn from you, too? You're no slouch yourself. You've got a lot to offer this (potential) kook, so say it loud and say it proud. If your guy is game to try your church for a change, read one of your favorite authors, or consider the healing benefits of country music, then he may not be this variety of kook. If your gal is open to exploring your method for doubling profits, how karate alters your body chemistry, or the wisdom of Yoda, she's probably not a Guru. Only time will tell, but if your lover is at all interested in your perspective on life, there's a good chance he or she is the real deal.

- **Take it Outside**

It's likely that you and your sweetie bonded over his or her belief system, self-improvement tapes, training course, religious community, or something that filled a void for you. Otherwise, you wouldn't be reading this chapter! It's also likely that whatever brought you two together is what you spend most of your time doing. Step outside of your routine and look for more common ground. Try new things together, something that brings out the novice in both of you. A true blue sweetie will go for it, and a Guru will either scoff at the idea or avoid the issue. And if your guy or gal is just lightly Guru-like, it may be just what he or she needs to stop the kook train from picking up speed.

- **Check Yourself**

Are you giving up too much of yourself? Do you resemble your old self at all? What do you do for fun and when was the last time you made time for it? If you suspect that you're dating a Guru, I would say you already know you are. But if you can't give up this guy or gal, then you need to make sure you don't lose yourself completely.

Check in with yourself on a regular basis, just to make sure you're still in there somewhere. See old, trusted friends and get their read on you – not him – *you*. Dust off those old dreams, ideas, and desires and make sure they still have a place in your life, if you still want them. Loving a Guru means you must be hyper vigilant when it comes to maintaining your own identity, otherwise you just may end up swallowed whole.

The thing about loving a Guru is it feels so good all the way down. South, that is. You'll feel energized, important, hopeful, and proud. You'll walk with your head held high, with a renewed sense of purpose. You'll get a new wardrobe, make new friends; heck, you may even ditch that support group for good. But even though it feels so good, so good you're thinking, "There's no way this is going south," you are, most assuredly, going down.

Anytime you give up any authentic part of who you are for a lover who claims to know what's best for you, you are going to end up broken down and brokenhearted. And if you stay too long, it could take you years to remember who you once were. Remember, there is no give and take with this kook. You, the essence of you, is not important. You are just a piece of soapstone waiting for the Guru's expert sculpting hands. If you sign up for this life, you'll always be a shadow, a novice, or a ward. You'll never be you, authentically you.

So before you drink the Kool-aid, before you quit your job, lose all of your friends, or forget about your own aspirations entirely, find out if he or she loves you for who you are. It's easy to do. Just stop buying the BS and see what happens. The real Gurus will cut and run.

The Loafer

Carol said Dean's "apartment" turned out to be his parent's basement.

The Loafer is a common kook, so much so that most of us will date one at some point in our lives. The Loafer's that almost-perfect guy or gal with just one, nagging little problem: Still lives at home with Mommy and Daddy. Well, not *quite* almost-perfect. The thing is, the Loafers are nowhere near close to perfect no matter how loving, kind, sexy, or generous they appear to be. If your darling truly is a Loafer, he or she has a whole host of problems that you may not yet realize and that you most certainly cannot fix.

What makes the Loafers kooks is their inability to live in the real world, taking on the normal responsibilities the rest of us grown-ups deal with every day. Rent. Groceries. Car insurance. Basic household tasks. She's the gal who still needs Daddy to pay her credit card bill every month. He's the guy who still hangs out with his high school buddies and has no desire to make new friends. She's the gal who won't lift a finger to help in the kitchen. He's the guy who doesn't know how to do his own laundry. The Loafer is the kook who doesn't want to grow up.

The Loafer, who is also often the Lost, or the Baby, or a combination of the two, is happy living at home. Why not? Doesn't have to worry about what to make for dinner (or how to pay for it), never has to look at a water bill (or even knows what it looks like), and generally has no idea of how to make it on his or her own (and doesn't think this is a problem).

If you're dating a Loafer, don't think for a minute that the loafing ways will move out once the Loafer has moved in with you. Be prepared to pay all the bills, do all of the cleaning, and make all of the plans, because the Loafer sure doesn't know how. What you see now is what you get later. Are you ready for that?

X + Y = A Whole Generation of Kooks?

According to a 2006 report from the U.S. Census Bureau, more than thirty-four million adult children between the ages of 25 and 44 still live at home, and that number has likely gone up. Yikes! Do we have an entire generation – or two – of kooks? Because it sure looks as though Generation X and Generation Y have opted to hang at the homestead rather than make their own way.

Do we have an epidemic of Loafers on our hands? Could be. But at least some part of the equation has to do with the economy. Within these numbers are well-educated individuals drowning under student loans, working hard toward the goal of finally getting out of their childhood home. There are also men and women who returned home after downsizing or divorce got the better of them, but they, too, view their situation as only temporary. Still more of this number are grown-ups who are priced out of the housing market and can't even afford rent (think New York City, San Francisco, etc.) – yet.

The key distinction here is that all of these people a) want to get out of their parents' house and b) have a plan to do precisely that. Not the Loafer, who has a good thing going and has no plans to move anytime soon. The Loafer lacks direction and doesn't see a problem with that. Worse (for you), he or she has no possibility of a mature relationship with a partner. That requires privacy and independence to develop and cohabitation to deepen. But again, the Loafer doesn't see it that way.

So is your guy or gal a Loafer or simply "in between?" Let's find out, shall we?

My Dumpling Just Needs To Get Back on His or Her Feet

It might be true. It is possible. Your dumpling could be living at home in order to save enough money to start again. But what if Dumpling never really left home? Before you say anything, going away to college doesn't count. We all know it's just high school with beer, a cocoon-like environment where people offer you guidance and you don't punch a clock or pay utilities. If your partner has never had an apartment or house of his or her own, he or she hasn't gotten "knocked down" yet, either.

But let's say your dumpling did and has. Your guy or gal left home, made a life, and then got kicked in the proverbial teeth. Is Dumpling really living with his or her folks until the wounds and the bank account heal, or is Dumpling thinking of staying...forever? Some people can't hack it in the real world and are crippled by the normal knocks and bruises we all handle just fine on our own (with the occasional help from mood-altering substances). Others take refuge in home and are paralyzed with fear over returning to the "real world." Whatever the reason, there's a good chance that your mate has *become* a Loafer.

Practically speaking, even if your guy or gal is *not* a Loafer but still can't manage to make it on his or her own, it is a situation to take very, very seriously. Perhaps your guy has kids with his ex and pays so much child support he cannot even hope to afford his own place in the next decade. Maybe your gal charged $80,000 in credit card debt and now just works to pay off the interest.

If your sweetie is still at home, you need to find out a) how Sweetie got there, b) if it's economically feasible for Sweetie to move out in the near future, and c) if Sweetie ever really left in the first place.

Welcome to the Family

Momma's boy. Daddy's girl. Remember, it takes two to tango – or in this case, to loaf. In order for your darling to pull off eternal childhood, he or she first has to have a willing parent or two. This good news is many parents would do just about anything to get their adult kids out of the house. The bad news is some parents are perfectly content to let their kid live with them indefinitely.

If you're dating a Loafer, you're going to have to deal with the family from the get go. Did you really want to be this involved with your sweetie's family this early in your relationship? Or, if you're already in love, do you really want to be enmeshed in the family dramas *before* you say, "I do?" Dating a Loafer means you get to spend a lot of quality time with "the family." A lot. Are you ready to meet the parents, *and* see them every day?

If by some miracle your kook becomes inspired to leave the nest and feather a new one with you, are you prepared for the fallout from the folks? The sad truth is it isn't just the Loafer who has trouble moving on. Some mommies and daddies just can't let go. Maybe you two could convert the garage and call it a "starter home." So what if it doesn't have its own bathroom? You don't mind sharing, right?

Why Do Loafers Do It?

Simply put, the Loafers are scared to grow up. Even if they returned home from college or a failed attempt to join the real world, these kooks really never left home. Not emotionally, anyway. It was only a matter of time before they came back, duffle bag in hand, asking Mom and Dad if they could have the old room back.

Life is hard and sometimes scary, so why do any of us ever leave home? Because we want to make our own lives. We want to start our own families, carve out our own careers, and find our place in the world. We're all just a little bit scared to take that first step and fill out that application for our first apartment. But we do it. Because we know that on the other side of the fear, there is great reward. Independence.

The Loafers don't want to be independent. They're lazy and scared and set in their ways. They have yet to grow up and do not intend to try. How can you possibly expect a long-term commitment from an overgrown child?

Let Me Be Your Guide (or Why YOU Do It)

So how did you end up with a modern-day Peter Pan on your hands? Easy. You like playing "parent." Some part of you enjoys the fact that the Loafer has yet to launch, and you want to be the one to help him or her do it. You see your future in-laws as deficient in some way, unable to properly guide their child into adulthood. You think, if his or her parents weren't so accommodating and/or controlling, my honey would be out of there like that! (You should imagine me snapping my fingers for effect!)

It's true: As long as your Loafer's parents continue to provide a safe haven with absolutely no expectation of an end date, he or she is not going to be motivated to move. But that's not necessarily the parents' fault (though it does aggravate the situation). It's because *your partner's a Loafer* - has a Loafer's mentality, *doesn't want to move out*, is not being held against his or her will, is perfectly content. So as much as you want to be the one that helps this kook move out and move on, it's not going to happen.

But if by some miracle (not you, Honey) the Loafer *does* decide to call U-Haul, be prepared. This kook doesn't know how to do ANYTHING on his or her own. Are you getting a mental picture of life with a Loafer post-Mom-and-Dad? Not a pretty vision, is it?

How to Spot the Loafer

The first clue that you are dating a Loafer is that he or she lives with the folks. But you need to gather more evidence before you can definitively conclude that your guy or gal is this variety of kook. Here are three HUGE clues that your sweetie is a Loafer. If Sweetie has one or two of the qualities, Sweetie is probably a Loafer. If Sweetie has all three qualities, take your cues from the great game of baseball and say, "You're out!"

- **No Responsibilities**

Does your partner help around the house, or do the parents take care of everything? Does she expect Mom and Dad to do all of the cooking, cleaning, maintenance, and shopping? Does he at least do his own laundry and pick up his own messes? Or do the folks pay the bills, fix the problems, and make the plans for your lover, so that he or she doesn't have to lift a finger?

If your guy or gal has no responsibilities or refuses to take on any responsibilities around the home, you may be in love with a Loafer. At the very least, your beloved is inconsiderate and lazy. Know this: Whatever the Loafer neglects at his or her own home, the Loafer will neglect at your home as well.

- **No Career**

Does your guy or gal have a dedicated career or jump from job to job? Does he work as a temp, a retail sales associate, or take orders at the drive-through? Is she "between jobs" most of the time, with no real interest in finding one? Does he seem to have little gumption when it comes to work and no interest in finding a rewarding position with decent pay and benefits?

If your dreamboat seems to have the work ethic of a three-toed sloth, you may have found yourself a Loafer. This kook is not good at holding down a job and has very little motivation to do so. It's just pocket money, anyway, right? Just enough cash for dates, video games, shoes, and that annual trip to Fort Lauderdale to relive Spring Break

'91. Again, don't think that just because your darling changes zip codes that he or she will be able to contribute financially in any significant way. The person who left Mom's and Dad's is the same one who's coming to your pad; nothing changed along the way. If you're serious about this one, better ask Mommy and Daddy how much they kick in and figure out if you can afford it, too.

- **No Plans**

Does your sweetie seem to have a goal of finishing college, or moving up at the ranks at work, or paying off debt, in order to get out of the parents' home? Or does he or she seem to have no plans to move out in the near – or faraway – future? Is Sweetie stowing away any savings or living paycheck to paycheck, charging up credit cards and ignoring student loans? Are there frivolous purchases using part-time pay? When you talk about the future, does Sweetie envision a different life from the current one or just a *different version* of it?

If your cutie pie has no plans to move out, he or she also has no desire to move out. Desire leads to goals, and goals lead to plans. Tasks. A to-do list. A calendar of activities that moves one further towards one's goal. By the way, *you* are not enough of a reason for the Loafer to move out. The Loafer needs to find that desire deep inside, so that he or she can make the necessary lifestyle and behavioral changes to see it through.

One quick note about the loafing kook: Not all Loafers live at home. Some live off of their parents but at a separate address. Perhaps Mom and Dad have a rental unit and allow your guy or gal to stay rent-free. Or maybe Mom and Dad are *paying* the rent on your sweetie's pad, thereby allowing your kook to loaf about indefinitely. Find out. It may seem like a sweet deal, but if you stick around long enough to say, "I do" it can only mean trouble.

What if I'm Not Sure?

Frankly, I'm a little surprised that you're not sure if your guy or gal is a Loafer. The signs are very obvious and hard to hide. Still, if you're honestly still not sure, here are the last remaining reasons why your sweetie might be living at home:

- **Recovering From an Illness or Injury**

If your partner is ill, or is recovering from an illness or injury, or recently recovered from an illness or injury and is starting over again, living with Mom and Dad is perfectly natural. I'm not talking about the flu here, people, or even mono; I'm talking about a chronic or life-threatening illness, or a serious injury, that requires care and time and kisses from Mommy.

- **Caring for Parents**

Many adults move back in with their parents in order to care for them rather than send either or both to a nursing home. It could be a temporary situation, such as a post-surgery or post-injury recovery period. Or it could be a long-term situation, such as Alzheimer's, requiring your partner to attend to his or her parent(s) indefinitely. This has its own set of challenges, but it's not kooky. It's kind of your love to sacrifice for the 'rents, and it shows a sense of responsibility and duty. Qualities the Loafer does not have or refuses to cultivate.

- **Still in College**

College is expensive, and paying for housing on top of tuition and books can be prohibitive for many people. If your guy or gal is returning to college late in life, this may mean quitting a job, and so moving back in with Mom and Dad may be the only option. Still, if your partner is still in college and living at home, do find out if he or she has been in school for years and years. You may have a Loafer (or a Lost) disguised as a professional student.

- **Family Culture**

In many cultures, it is perfectly normal, if not expected, for the unmarried adult children to remain at home with their parents until that big wedding day. If your guy or gal comes from a culture that requires such staying at home, I wouldn't worry about it. However, while your beloved probably isn't a Loafer, I would pay close attention to what is expected of him or her in the home environment. If Beloved helps out financially but couldn't boil water to save his or her life, expect nothing more (or less) in your own home.

The problem with the Loafers isn't really that they live in the basement of their parents' house, it's that they *like* living in the basement of their parents' house. They're just hanging out, content to let Mom and Dad take care of everything until the end of time. Aside from the fact that they are woefully ill-prepared for the real world – which they will have to enter at some point – the Loafers can't relate to those who actually live in it. Without this common experience, how are you to achieve a sense of togetherness, that special feeling that it's you two against the world?

The Loafer has no direction, no plans, no goals, and no aspirations beyond the Fall television lineup. By nature, the Loafer is also selfish, lazy, and afraid of commitment. Tasty. Can you get past all of this? Not likely. At least not without a lot of patience on your part, and hard work on his or her part. Which, again, isn't likely.

If you do manage to wrestle the Loafer from the comforts of the parental home, get ready for a long, frustrating road full of disappointment, resentment, and, eventually, regret. Because the Loafer will always loaf no matter if it's on Mom's couch – or yours.

The Lost

Arthur said Danielle changed her major five times before she finally dropped out of college and took a temp job.

Unlike many of the personalities described in this book, The Lost is a kook without a plan. There is no carefully planned approach to get you into the sack or down the aisle, no well-honed system for avoiding commitment or stealing your hard-earned cash. The Lost is just that. Lost. Lacking direction. Bouncing around from job to job, city to city, hobby to hobby.

With feet that rarely touch the ground, the Lost is not rooted to anything or anyone, and so in many ways this kook seems like a breath of fresh air – someone who has a lot of time for you and fits seamlessly into your life. The Lost has no trouble juggling or even canceling plans to accommodate your busy schedule. It's as if this kook is a rare, budding flower who just happens to be in love with you. The possibilities are endless.

It takes very little arm-twisting to get the Lost to pull up stakes and change course to walk your path with you. He or she is more than willing to consider relocating to Malawi for two years while you conduct research for your thesis or switch jobs to be closer to your apartment. But this person would also quit that same job in order to road-trip with a group of college buddies. He'll spend $500 on a home-real-estate course and then never get beyond tape one. She will give up, start over, change direction, and dive in again at a moment's notice and often for no good reason.

While the Lost seems like an attentive lover, an amenable partner, and the perfect solution to your busy life and schedule, he or she really is an all-consuming project waiting to happen. Initially, this lovable kook will respond to your gentle persuasion, your subtle hints and bright ideas. But eventually the Lost will let you down by switching gears or donning concrete shoes, and you'll soon realize you've fallen for someone who may *never* get it together. At that point you have to ask yourself, is this person the love of my life, or my life's work?

You're the Inspiration

"You're the meaning in my life, you're the inspiration.

You bring feeling to my life, you're the inspiration."

I know what you're thinking. Why am I quoting the syrupy 80s band, *Chicago*? Because it's a perfect example of how we welcome the Lost into our lives. Just as we may outwardly shun Peter Cetera ballads to our sophisticated friends, we secretly sing along whenever his songs come on the radio. The songs sneak up on us and hook us where it counts: Our need to be somebody's entire world.

The Lost are experts at convincing us that all they need is to be inspired. It's not that they're not driven; they just haven't found that elusive "thing" that motivates other people – like you – to keep a job, make a plan, and follow through. That is, until you came along.

The reason the Lost are so good at making us feel like we're the answers to their prayers? Because they *believe* it to be true. It's not that they are (consciously) manipulating us; they genuinely believe that we can fill in all of the blanks. Finally, your own personal Lost has found in you the anchor for his boat, the road map for her journey. And that, my friend, is stronger than love potion number nine, ten, and eleven put together. You'll have a hard time getting past the allure of being someone's muse to see the lost soul underneath.

We Balance Each Other Perfectly

It's likely that if you have hooked up with a Lost kook, it's a case of opposites attract. Polar opposites, even. When you're mired down in work, he whisks you away for an impromptu picnic lunch. When you're worried about making your house payment, she helps you calm down and reflect on all that you have. You're driven and organized, he's relaxed and curious; you're prompt, she is of the moment.

But while opposites attract, they don't always fit. The Online Dictionary defines the term "polar opposite" as, "That which is conspicuously different in most important respects." *Conspicuously different in most important respects.* Does that sound like a good foundation on which to build a life?

Even if you're not that different from your very own Lost kook, you wouldn't be together if your needs and his or her needs were not being met in some fashion. We often seek in others what we need to change the most in ourselves. So if you need to chill out a bit, or get the gumption to follow a dormant dream, falling for a Lost may be just the impetus you need to balance your own personality. Likewise, the Lost may need a dose of practical application, a little "how-to" inspiration and a living example for how to knuckle down and get things done.

But again, is this enough to keep you going "until death do us part?" Are you prepared for the ups and downs of life with the Lost? Could you be the primary breadwinner – forever? Would you be able to summon the same genuine enthusiasm for every new career or business idea your guy comes up with? Are you willing to face a stack of student loan bills from different colleges or the "in between" weeks or months when you're schlepping off to work and your sweetie is trying to find herself?

Maybe you are and maybe you can. But don't forget that our society does not support the Lost lifestyle. Eventually, the lack of direction takes its toll on even the most dedicated Lost kook, and he or she may develop depression, anxiety, or any number of conditions borne of a lifetime of not measuring up to the standards of others. So yes, you do adore your sweetie's free spirit *and* struggle, but even if you can get past the fact that there is nothing you can do to motivate a change in Sweetie's wandering ways, can you deal with the changes in him or her when Sweetie realizes the whole world thinks he or she is a loser?

Why Do the Lost Do It?

Lack of direction could be a sign of poor self-esteem, an absence of confidence, or a fear of failure. The Lost could be plagued with any number of psychological scars that prevent them from committing to any one pursuit. To some extent, all of us question our worth, distrust our capability, and worry we will fail. It is not uncommon to fear the unknown. But what should be a temporary feeling, or at least a feeling we can push through, is actually a brick wall for the Lost.

Of course, there are some Lost who really are another kook in disguise (as is so often the case). You could have a deadbeat on your hands, a slacker more interested in time off than working hard. (See previous chapter.) Your kook could appear to be lacking in direction but, in fact, really just doesn't *want* to have direction.

Dating a Lost kook can also be confusing, because he or she may not necessarily have the same problem with relationships. Your guy or gal may be perfectly ready to file jointly and may not have any issue with working through any number of marital peaks and valleys. So it's not that the Lost is a *total* slacker. Just in every way but one.

On the other hand, your Lost kook may not even *be* a slacker. It could be that your darling has a bona fide medical condition that prevents him or her from setting and focusing on goals. I'm referring to adult Attention Deficit Disorder, or ADD. Much has been written about ADD, and there are many dissenting opinions. In fact, some believe the disorder doesn't really exist. These are the "pull up your bootstraps" variety of psychologists and psychiatrists. What those who believe ADD exists will tell you is that it is virtually impossible for someone with ADD to pull up those straps.

In his book, *Delivered from Distraction: Getting the Most out of Life with Attention Deficit Disorder*, Edward M. Hallowell, M.D., who has ADD himself, has this to say about what it's like to have ADD:

> Your brain goes faster than the average brain. Your trouble is putting on the brakes. You get one idea and you have to act on it, and then, what do you know, but you've got another idea before you've finished up the first one, and so you go for that one, and pretty soon people are calling you disorganized and impulsive and disobedient and defiant and all sorts of impolite words that miss the point completely. Because you're trying so hard to get it right. It's just that you have all these invisible vectors pulling you this way and that, which makes it really hard to stay on task. (page number from book.)

Not all Lost kooks have ADD. But if your honey does have ADD, count your many blessings because he or she is NOT a kook. Remember, the American Heritage Dictionary defines a kook as, "A person regarded as strange, eccentric, or crazy." Having ADD does not make you any of those things. Of course, you could be a kook *and* have ADD, but if you have a Lost kook on your hands who really has ADD, there's hope. There are various treatments that can help people with ADD, and so that lovely person who would be perfect if he or she could just get his or her life together may, in fact, be your dreamboat. Dreamboat just might need a little (professional) help sorting it all out.

Everyone Loves a "Fixer Upper" (or Why YOU Do It)

Knocked Up. My Fair Lady. Pretty Woman. All of these are movies in which one person renovates body, mind or soul, motivated and/or guided by the perfect love. The list of films and stories that I would call "fixer uppers" is long, and that is because as entertainment consumers, we find this type of story very satisfying. It thrills us to watch a character's complete transformation, usually to great reward. The same is true for underdog movies, usually centered on sports or competition. We root for the team that, against all odds, pulls off the win and takes home the prize.

If you love fixer-upper and underdog stories, chances are you can't resist when a great looking "before" comes waltzing into your life. You get excited at the thought of helping him land a great new job – and an awesome haircut. You get a charge out of giving her advice about a new career path – and then paying for the classes. Well, I've got news for you. You're not Jenny Craig or Simon Cowell. No amount of love, patience, or brilliant planning can rescue the Lost from themselves.

You, my friend, want to be Henry Higgins. (The professor in *My Fair Lady* for all of you non-musical types.) As much as you love your pumpkin, the thought of helping Pumpkin find his or her North Star is an intoxicating challenge that can't be ignored. Some part of you wants to be able to take credit for your sweetie's success.

That was Henry's fatal flaw, too. And might I remind you that Henry Higgins got dumped? After he successfully transformed Eliza Doolittle from a lowly street urchin into a cultured, sophisticated lady, she kicked him to the curb. You see, no one really wants to be molded into something new. People just want to be loved. Can you do that? Can you love your Lost kook for who he or she is?

How to Spot the Lost

The Lost are interesting people. They might have friends in every major city (because they've lived in all of them), they may have many great stories about a wide variety of experiences (because they've tried them), but they have very few tokens of accomplishment (because they bailed before they could obtain them). Spotting these kooks requires identification of other personality traits, such as these:

- **The Dabbler**

If your beloved is a dabbler, you may have a Lost kook on your hands. An expert in nothing, the dabbler has a little bit of knowledge about a lot of things. She seems to follow whims, changing schools, jobs, and even careers at the drop of a hat. Listen closely. You might hear words like, "My new job," or, "When I was a _____ (beautician, bookkeeper, building manager)." You'll hear references to the various experiences your kook has had, and it won't be long before you realize she is not really a worldly free spirit. She is, in fact, lost.

Dabblers may also have a lot of unfinished projects lying around the house. Your guy has only half of his bathroom tiles pulled up, which he did sometime last year. Your gal has $2,000 worth of paints, brushes, and canvas stacked up in the living room for an art class she stopped attending after three weeks. Look around. If your guy or gal has a plethora of "I'll-get-to-that-soon" projects in plain view (or hidden away), you may have spotted the Lost.

- **The Gypsy**

Gypsies have mementos and stories from every place they've ever lived. Photos of friends in faraway places, trinkets from big cities, small towns, communes, wherever. Your gal went to Santa Fe on vacation and loved it so much she stayed for two years. Your guy prides himself on having only enough stuff to fit in his car – just in case he wants to move. Gypsies can be their own kooks – commitment-phobes and thrill seekers – but they can also just be your garden variety Lost. After all, what would be a great way to erase all memory of a disappointing career move? Start fresh and move someplace new!

- **The Choke Artist**

The choke artist is someone who sticks with something *almost* all the way but chokes just before reaching the finish line. Lost kooks are often also choke artists and so have many near wins under their belt. Usually, there was some sort of seemingly insurmountable obstacle in the way; the choke artist rarely takes credit for dropping the ball. He's the guy who says he couldn't finish his degree because of personality conflicts with his professors. She's the gal who came down with a sudden case of mono just days before she had to audition for that television pilot.

Not everyone who flakes under pressure is a Lost kook, and certainly not every Lost is a choke artist. But if you are dating one or the other, there's a decent chance you are dating both.

What if I'm Not Sure?

It's hard to accept you have handed your heart to a Lost. There is always that chance that your honey might soon see the light, and you hold on to that possibility like white on rice. There are a few things you can do to find out how severe – or permanent – your sweetie's lack of direction is, strategies that would effectively remove you from the equation. Because if your Lost has won your heart, the first thing you must do is stop trying to be his or her compass.

- **Suggest Therapy**

Lost kooks rarely go to therapy – that would require a long-term commitment. But do test the waters and recommend therapy to your sweetheart. Okay. I know this is not exactly romantic dinner conversation, but you could offer to go as well (if you're not already in therapy). If your sweetheart refuses to go, or goes once and then quits, you probably have at least one type of kook on your hands.

- **Find a Life Coach**

If therapy sounds too daunting, suggest a life coach. Geared more toward immediate results and goal achievement, the life coach gets it done. If your darling is truly a Lost, he or she may actually benefit from working with a life coach. A coach has less of a stigma than a therapist, and it still keeps you out of it. Most life coaches use behavior modification tricks rather than deep healing, and that may be just what the doctor ordered.

- **Set Your Own Deadlines**

You have your own goals and dreams. Remember? You've been quite busy holding your sweetie's hand, and you've let your own aspirations fade into the background. With all of your time and energy focused on your guy or gal, you rarely have enough left over to complete your own tasks. That has to stop because a) setting your own plans aside only breeds resentment in an otherwise loving relationship and b) you will NEVER have enough stamina, bright ideas, or words of inspiration to get the Lost to follow through. It's sad to lose the one you love, but it's a damn tragedy to lose your dreams in the process.

It's easy to get wrapped up in the misadventures of a Lost. Most of us want to help our lovers and friends. We derive satisfaction from aiding people in need, providing them with guidance and encouragement. But if you need your partner to help pay the mortgage, eventually your desire to help him or her will be replaced with a desperate need to fix him or her, and that will ultimately lead to a deeply rooted resentment. That's not going to keep the fires burnin', trust me.

If you're going to love a Lost, you better love that kook the way he or she is now. Because unless there is a medical condition that can be treated or divine intervention occurs, what you see is what you get.

The Love Lover

Cathy said Tim was so in love with being in love that he had been engaged fifteen times!

Warning: These kooks can really break your heart. The Love Lover is especially dangerous because they feed into all of our romantic notions of love, the stuff we dream about on lonely Saturday nights. The chance encounter, the intense gaze, the feeling of love at first sight. The Love Lover has 'em all wrapped up in a pretty package that's hard to refuse.

Thanks to American films, we are susceptible to romantic fantasies about being in love. The Love Lovers not only yearn for it, they need it. The first blush of love is what the Love Lover is all about, the early weeks and months when you are consumed with thoughts of your new lover and both of you are perfect in every way.

The Love Lover has a powerful urge to sustain the feeling of being swept away by new love, but we all know that romantic love grows into real, true love. The kind of love that gets you through hard times and new babies, deepening over time *because* of the storms you weathered together. The Love Lover wants nothing to do with this deeper love, wants only the first spark, the tingles, the daydreaming, and, of course, the constant sex.

It's not hard to see the end of this tale. Because it's impossible to sustain that level of intensity in any relationship, the Love Lover will eventually grow tired of you and break off all of your dreamy plans in search of a new, new love. In fact, your love affair with the Love Lover can be over and done with in as little as one week, during which time you will have been so caught up in the amorous, romantic declarations that you will have already named your future children.

Love Lover or Romantic Fool?

It feels like love, this enchanting emotion that causes you to consider giving up your dream job and relocating to Florida just to be with your Love Lover. But it really isn't.

It's romance. Granted, it's an awesome romance that makes you feel as though you've found *the one*, but it's still just hearts, flowers and champagne.

I'm not knocking romance. It's good stuff. It gets you together with your dreamboat and carries you through the early stages of a new relationship when his remote control obsession or her shoe buying habit might have otherwise turned you off. When you're in the romance stage, you just think all of those idiosyncrasies are cute. Later, when you finally notice and become annoyed, you're in the real love stage and won't let something small – albeit annoying – break up your happy union.

So the Love Lover is really in love with romantic feelings. This kook doesn't really want to know you at all, not the real you anyway. Just the romantic you, the one that creeps out of bed early for a quick tooth brushing before he or she wakes up. Yeah. Like you're going to be doing that every morning for the rest of your life.

The American Heritage Dictionary defines romance as, "A strong, sometimes short-lived attachment, fascination, or enthusiasm for something." There are other definitions, such as, "A love affair" and, my favorite, "An ardent emotional attachment or involvement between people." Sound familiar? If you're one of the notches on the Love Lover's bedpost, I'm sure these definitions ring true. The Love Lover may call it love, but if it catches fire and burns out quickly, it's romance, pure and simple.

Why Do Love Lovers Do It?

While I can't tell you the unique reasons why your very own Love Lover may be avoiding reality, I am quite certain that he or she *is* avoiding reality. It's more than just a distaste for "getting real" with a partner. The Love Lover doesn't want to get real with the one in the mirror.

Gary Zukav, author of *Seat of the Soul* and *Soul Stories*, puts it this way: "Romance is your desire to make yourself complete through another person rather than through your own inner work," (page number in book). In other words, the Love Lover is using YOU to avoid dealing with his or her own issues.

This is heavy, complicated psychology, and you are not the person for the job. No matter how wonderful you are, you cannot convert the Love Lover into a steady date, much less a lifelong companion. The Love Lover lives in a fantasy world, and the moment you stop playing your part (i.e. have expectations, disagree over an issue, etc.), it's time to let you go and search for a new player.

There is at least one other reason why the Love Lover chooses a Don Juan existence over meeting Mom and Dad: The breakup from hell. It's quite possible your perpetual hot date is trying to protect a battered heart from future flesh wounds. He may have been blindsided by love and, as a result, developed a firmly rooted belief that *real* relationships are for losers. She may also harbor a deep resentment toward any object of her affection and so withholds and withdraws when things get too serious.

If a broken heart is behind your kook's kookiness, keep on moving. I know you *want* to believe you can kiss it and make it all better. You probably get a thrill at the notion that you could be the one who helped your dreamboat learn to love again. Guess what? You've seen too many movies. You can't heal someone else, and you'll make yourself crazy trying. Join an animal rescue squad and save wounded birds and puppies instead. They'll be much more grateful than the Love Lover ever would be. Loyal, too.

Gobsmacked! (Or Why YOU Do It)

You know why you do it. It's exhilarating, all-consuming, dreamy fun. You're singing along to sappy love songs, texting smooch updates to all your friends, starting a secret love blog in honor of the one you've been waiting for. You're hooked because new love takes you out of your life and into another dimension, one in which you're gorgeous and smart and life is generally perfect. You're smitten because when you're in love, you feel superhuman. Well, that and all the hot, sweaty sex. Kitchen table sex. Car sex. Outdoor sex. Yup. Anywhere and everywhere.

No one on earth would blame you for riding this love train, least of all me. It's chemistry. You can't fight it. And you don't want to try. When we fall in love, part of the allure is seeing ourselves through the eyes of our sweetie. The fact that Sweetie thinks you're a freaking genius makes you feel like you can do anything. No one in his or her right mind would pass that up.

Why you believe what the Love Lover says is something else entirely. Most of us have an inner censor that warns us when we're going too far, too fast. We want to pledge our undying love on the second date, but instinctively we know it's best to hold it in until we know a little bit more about the person. So why do you place your tender heart in a pretty box and hand it over so quickly? Sounds pretty kooky to me. Think about it.

How to Spot the Love Lover

Fortunately, the Love Lovers are easy ones to spot. They're intense, devoted, and make you feel like you're walking on air. Pretty easy to pick out, right? Here are some other personality traits and habits of the Love Lover to aid you in your efforts to spot this kook:

- **Faster Than a Speeding Bullet**

Superheroes they're not, but boy, the Love Lovers move fast. If you met at a party on Friday night, she would text you before breakfast on Saturday morning. On the first date, he tells you that you "might be the one;" by the fifth date, you're making plans for the future.

Even if I'm off by a few dates, you can spot Love Lovers by their telltale lack of boundaries and willingness to commit to a total stranger. After all, even if you are soul mates, you're still mere friendly acquaintances if you haven't yet met Mom!

- **Your Very Own Santa**

One of the ways you can distinguish Love Lovers from Agendas is by their romantic gestures. Flowers, jewelry, poems, and other love talismans play a part in every new relationship, but if your honey goes a bit overboard on the gift giving, it's a sign that he or she is too caught up in the moment and may not be in it for the long haul.

Every gift is significant, but that's especially the case in the early stages of a relationship. We wonder, should I buy him this? Will he think I'm too clingy? If I buy her jewelry, will it scare her away? Even the type of flowers we choose sends a message to the receiver.

A Love Lover throws all caution to the wind and never thinks about the implications of outrageous generosity. After all, it was love at first sight and you were meant to be, so why wait to give you a tangible demonstration of that love, even if it is six dozen red roses – and a key to his or her pad.

Giving gifts also increases the intensity of the "in love" feelings, creating more cinematic moments the Love Lover can't seem to get enough of. How much is too much? You'll know when it happens. You'll feel slightly uncomfortable accepting it, wondering what it means and if you're moving too fast. These questioning thoughts are usually fleeting, but if they pop up, take them as a sign that you may have found yourself a Love Lover.

- **Constant Companion**

When you're in love with the romance of being in love, you need to get your fix often and in large quantities. The Love Lover amazes you at first, because he or she *does* want to spend every waking moment with you. But do you really need someone to hold your hand while you walk to the bathroom?

The Love Lover is your constant companion, sending you dozens of text messages while you're at work, calling your cell, your work line, and your home line in the same day. If you're not chatting online, your Love Lover is sending you email declarations of love.

We all know what it's like to want to be with the new love of your life all of the time, so how can you tell it's too much? When those attentive emails and phone calls start to annoy you, it's a good sign. If you start to feel nervous when accepting an invitation to hang out with your friends, you may have a Love Lover on your hands. Of course, these traits can apply to other kooks, and stalkers, but the Love Lover is known for dedicating all of his or her time to you.

- **Too Many Exes**

Love Lovers are not in it for the long haul, and since they need a new love to feel good, it stands to reason they will have a whole catalog of exes. Of course, a lot of exes could mean your new darling is just a player, or unlucky in love, but doesn't that raise concern as well?

How many is too many? I think you know. Add up your honey's dating years (subtract high school – it doesn't count) and then divide the total by the number of exes you know about. Are there more than two exes per year? Remember, dalliances don't count, love affairs do. If your one and only has had more than two intense, committed relationships for every one of his or her dating years, you've got a Love Lover.

Actually, if there is an average of one per year, you probably have a Love Lover or some other kook on your hands. But I didn't want to scare you right away, so I went with two!

What if I'm Not Sure?

Is it possible that your muffin is *not* a Love Lover, even if Muffin has many of the personality traits we've discussed? Sure. There's always hope. If you're not positive you are dating a Love Lover, take these simple steps to protect yourself:

- **Slow Down**

Taking things slow will usually trip up any Love Lover, so by shifting gears a bit you may be able to spot the kook. More importantly, you will have protected your heart. While you may want to say, "Yes," when your honey asks you to move in, move away, or move on down the aisle, "Maybe," is a better answer until you're absolutely sure.

- **Don't Sign ANYTHING**

Please, please, one thousand times please, do not sign anything until you have been with your new love long enough to know his or her credit rating, marital status, child count (which includes the monthly amount of payment to the ex), and if he or she owes money to ANYONE. A broken heart can be mended, but a "broken" credit rating can take years to fix.

- **Keep it Real**

If you think you might be dating a Love Lover, be yourself. Lay off any pretensions designed to keep your sweetie in your favor, and "come as you are." If your Sweetie is a Love Lover, his or her true colors will emerge soon enough.

Love Lovers are first-rate kooks with romantic declarations and plenty of movie moments in their back pockets. It's easy to get caught up in the love tornado they create. Who of us doesn't want to be swept off of our feet?

Me, that's who. I want my feet planted firmly on the ground, thank you very much. Now my head, my head can be in the clouds, but I like to be able to run when I spot a kook!

Look, you're gorgeous and going places, you don't need what this kook's offering. It's not just a tired cliché – there really *are* plenty of fish in the sea. Enjoy the sex. By all means, enjoy the sex. But don't get sucked in to the Love Lover's game. She's not real. He's a mirage. They can't even be honest with themselves. How can you expect a Love Lover to be honest with you?

The Narcissist

Peter said Josh gave him affection only when Peter complimented him.

The Narcissist is completely consumed with ego, which needs regular stroking from, well, everyone. More than just vain, this kook needs to feel special, important, and powerful in every aspect of life. At work, with family, in relationships, at the gym – even in the bedroom. Obsessed with his or her own worth, the Narcissists are bottomless pits of need, requiring more and more praise, reassurance, and accolades as evidence of their unique beauty, superior brainpower, and awesome talents.

Psychologists believe narcissism varies in degrees, that it is a continuum with mild cases of egomania at one end of the spectrum and severe narcissistic personality disorder at the other end. Because of the wide range of traits, you could have a Narcissist in your life and not realize it.

Symptoms of narcissism may simply seem like minor annoyances to you, slipping through the cracks as you explain them away and get on with your day. But even if your partner's self-centeredness feels like something you can manage, you still may be dealing with a bona fide kook.

Your guy may be overly concerned with his appearance, and yours, as it pertains to him (of course). Your gal may run with the "in crowd" and view those who don't belong as peons that are not worthy of her time. Your guy talks over you, interrupting constantly, and always brings the conversation back to him. Your gal feels entitled to all of your time, money, and attention. The Narcissist is the kook who seeks out compliments, and pays attention to others only when they have something he or she wants or needs. Worst of all, the Narcissist has trouble with empathy. And by trouble, I mean the Narcissist doesn't have it. Fun. Really, fun.

The cold hard truth is that Narcissists can never truly be in love with you because they are already in love with someone else – themselves. Worse, their infatuation for you, which is actually an infatuation with how you *make them feel better about themselves*, can never ripen into the type of love that we all crave: true blue love. The kind of love that expands, shifts in shape and scope, and sticks with you and your partner until you both leave this earth. Nope. The Narcissist can't pull that off. Simply put, this kook will never love you the way you need to be loved.

Take it From the Greeks

A little Greek mythology never hurt anyone. In fact, the stories are designed to help mere mortals do right, gather courage, and work out their problems. So what did the Greeks hope to achieve in dreaming up Narcissus?

According to the myth, Narcissus was a beautiful young man who thought only of himself. All of the little nymphs were in love with him – think Zac Efron from *High School Musical* or, if you're from my crew, Johnny Depp or Rob Lowe. Very pretty and very crush-worthy. But despite his heartthrob status, Narcissus wasn't into the girls – or boys. He was into himself. He rejected all of his admirers and potential suitors, which eventually caused his downfall.

One of the spurned maidens prayed to the gods that Narcissus would experience what it felt like to be her, loving him and getting nothing in return. Her prayer was heard, and one day, when Narcissus was resting by the river, he fell in love with a gorgeous creature – his own reflection. Of course, he could not touch his love, for every time he tried, his own image disappeared. He died that way, staring at his own reflection. Narcissus forgot to take care of the basics (like eating and drinking water) as he gazed upon the most beautiful sight he had ever seen – himself.

The Greeks told this tale of death by vanity as a caution to egocentric individuals. An extreme example of the consequence of indulging our own narcissistic tendencies, this myth reminds us that obsessive love of self isn't healthy. It causes one to reject others and forget about the most basic requirements for a happy life. Are you sure you want to take this kook to the office Christmas party? Read on.

Punch line: You're the Mirror!

The tricky thing about dating Narcissists is that you may feel as though they are into you, but really, they are just staring back at themselves. Because you only serve one purpose: To reflect their own image and value. You're the river in the myth, the means by which Narcissus can gaze upon his own image. That makes you very necessary, and so the Narcissist will most likely do everything in his or her power to maintain the relationship. Unless you stop being the mirror.

When we fall in love with someone, some part of the equation is how that person looks at us, sees us. She loves your freckles (which you merely tolerate), and he worships at your big feet (which you consider your worst trait). She thinks you're brilliant, kind, and generous. He thinks you're hilarious, gorgeous, and talented. In falling in love with our new guy or gal, we are also, in part, falling in love with ourselves.

But the Narcissist does not offer it in return. When you're ready to move on to a deeper, more satisfying love, the Narcissist is still looking to you to confirm that he or she is awesome (stunning, powerful, all-knowing, omnipotent). You were more than forthcoming with compliments in the beginning (aren't we all?), and you certainly don't want to withhold them, but does your sweet pea really have to be THE topic of every conversation?

I'd like to point out that being a mirror for your sweetie can actually be a dangerous job. Pathological narcissists are prone to extreme, grandiose, sometimes delusional thinking. They want to be the best at something, and that might mean your guy or gal wants to be the most feared, the most notorious, or the most hated. He or she needs YOU to make that happen. And you thought you were just going for sushi!

But don't worry. Once you *stop* playing the game and refuse to act as a mirror for this kook, he or she will want out. When the Narcissist doesn't get what the Narcissist wants, you'll be dropped like an out-of-work reality TV star. Sad. So sad.

But Adryenn, Aren't We Supposed to Have Self-Esteem?

Ironic, isn't it? How many books on self-love, self-esteem, and self-care are on your bedside table? Thousands of books have been written on the subject of healthy self-esteem and how to get it, low self-esteem and how to raise it, and learning to love and care for yourself in order to achieve the life you dream about.

Yet here we are, talking about the dangers of *too much* self-love. If you're confused, take heart. It IS confusing. You want a guy who has ambition and walks tall or a gal who likes herself and takes pride in her appearance. Those are *good* traits, right? Aren't we supposed to go for confident, well-adjusted individuals with self-esteem?

Yup. You're right. No one wants to spend three hours, much less a lifetime, with someone who looks at life through a distorted, depressing filter and cannot see his or her own worth. But there is a difference between self-care and self-obsession. When you are working on improving your self-image, kind words, positive attention and accomplishment aid you on that journey. But the Narcissist never gets enough.

Does the Narcissist really have a wretched case of low self-esteem? Maybe. Maybe this kook is like someone with Prader-Willi Syndrome (a person who cannot stop eating) except is hungry for attention, accolades, and praise and can never be full. Who's got time for that?

Why Does The Narcissist Do It?

Before we dive into the reason why your guy or gal may exhibit narcissistic traits, let me first remind you that this problem varies in severity from person to person. In truth, we all have some of these tendencies some of the time. It's when the traits are extreme and constant, precluding normal actions and reactions between the Narcissist and the rest of the world, that this type of behavior is considered kooky.

As we discussed earlier, a Narcissist with otherwise normal psychological development may have a poor self-image and so requires constant praise and overcompensates with arrogance. On the other hand, a Narcissist may do what he or she does because of a driving ambition, a need to be the best in all things to the exclusion of everything and everyone else..

Although your sweetie may not be certifiable, I find it helps to look closely at Narcissistic Personality Disorder for clues about every grade of Narcissist. According to MayoClinic.com, there is no known cause of narcissism. However, it does provide a list of possible contributing factors related to parenting, including "excessive admiration that is never balanced with realistic feedback," "unpredictable or unreliable care giving from parents," and "severe emotional abuse in childhood." (For a complete list of possible causes of Narcissistic Personality Disorder, go to the Mental Health section at www.MayoClinic.com.)

Unless you are a psychotherapist, you are not qualified to diagnose your guy or gal, so best leave it to the pros. But in case you're curious, here's a list of nine traits of a Narcissist (also from the Mayo Clinic). If five or more of these traits are present in your sweetie, time to work out an exit strategy:

1. Envy of other people or a belief that you are the subject of other people's envy.
2. Exploitation of other people.
3. Fantasies about having exceptional qualities.
4. Grandiose self image.
5. Lack of empathy.
6. Need for excessive admiration.
7. Sense of being so special that only other special people can understand or relate to the individual.
8. Sense of entitlement.

Now I ask you, how hard do you think it would be to treat someone with Narcissistic Personality Disorder? Is it even possible? It's not for me to say, but do you really want to deal with someone so pathological? You may be asking yourself, "What did I see in this person?" May I suggest a different question? "What does this person see in me?" Hmmm...

I'm the One That You Want (or Why YOU Do It)

Have you ever had a crush on the un-gettable guy? Did you ever pine for the gal who wouldn't give you the time of day? Loving someone from afar is as much about the anticipation and fantasy as it is about the subject of your admiration. Getting involved with a Narcissist is a bit like this type of love, only much, much worse. Though you may have this person in your bed, he or she is just as un-gettable as the high school hunk and the model on the train. You could be married to a Narcissist *for years* and never win his or her heart.

So what does all of this say about you? Do you like the longing? Do you love the chase? Do you get off on self-deprivation, getting support from friends and family as the wounded bird? Tough questions, I know, and you might be pretty darned annoyed with me right now. But my friend, the Narcissist is not your everyday kook. The Narcissist is a master at manipulation and can have your head spinning around and your heart on the floor faster than you can say, "No, thank you."

We want to be our partner's soul mate, the only one. When you date a Narcissist, the need to get past his or her aloof demeanor, careless actions, and self-centered approach overpowers all sense of reason. If only we could get through to this otherwise wonderful person! Perhaps if I change my hair, my job, or my name? Maybe I should learn to walk slower, do more, and keep my mouth shut. Maybe *then* Wonderful will see what a wonderful person *I* am. Like Wonderful did in the beginning. Sound familiar?

How to Spot the Narcissist

Narcissists are tough to spot because the traits can be attributed to other personality disorders or just plain ignorance. These kooks also routinely contradict themselves, and their behavior may be difficult to predict based on past experience. Narcissists also have absolutely *no idea* that they are narcissistic. For example, I have a friend who was so fed up with her boyfriend, a class-A Narcissist, that she actually gave him a copy of a book about narcissists as a present. His response? "I know a lot of people just like this!" Okay then.

Here are a few clues to help you spot a Narcissist kook (not necessarily someone with Narcissistic Personality Disorder):

- **The Art of Conversation**

This trait is really two sides of one sword. At first, Narcissists are very good at carrying on a conversation. They listen to you, relate to you, and validate your experience. These kooks want to hear all about your life and then some and hang on every word you say.

But here's the other side of it: The Narcissists will eventually become the worst conversationalists you ever met! Once they have you hooked, you'll be hard-pressed to get in two words. Gone are the days when your opinion mattered. Now, only their opinions matter, and disagreeing with them is treated as a hurtful act. There is no debating a Narcissist because a) they always win, and b) they will do whatever it takes to make sure they win, and c) they always win!

The Narcissists have no interest in better communication, meeting you halfway, or coming to a mutual understanding. That would require an interest in your point of view and empathy for your feelings. The Narcissists don't really care, and the mistake the rest of us make is treating them as if "deep down they really care." They don't and they won't. Ever.

One way to sniff out Narcissists is to put them in a group setting where you know they will not be the center of attention. Perhaps a party in a friend's honor. Or maybe a dinner out with gregarious people who also naturally dominate conversation. If your guy or gal pouts, gets angry, and then blames you for putting him or her in that situation, chances are you've fallen for a Narcissist.

- **The Art of Gift Giving**

Narcissists are known for giving lousy gifts. Or no gifts at all. This kook very often completely forgets about birthdays, anniversaries, and even neglects to purchase something for you during major holidays. You would think the fact that he or she is getting gifts from others would remind your sweetie to pick up a tie or a bottle of perfume, but no.

Notorious for purchasing items for themselves, the Narcissists are easier to spot when you take all of their stuff into consideration. Did you get a used toaster oven for a gift – nine weeks late – while your guy spent a small fortune on tech toys? Were you presented with a $10 gift certificate to Starbucks after your gal bought $5,000 worth of shoes? (And you don't even like coffee!)

She was just so busy. He forgot. She's not into tangible demonstrations of love. He's a conservationist, not a materialist pig. Whatever the excuse, the Narcissist cannot be "trained" into becoming a generous, thoughtful person. So don't buy that book on how to do it!

- **The Art of the Apology**

The Narcissist will rarely, if ever, apologize. Lacking in empathy, it is impossible for this kook to feel remorse. When a Narcissist hurts you – and yours will eventually hurt you – there will be no comfort, no gentleness, and most certainly no apology. Instead, you will be sent on a mind trip from hell, one wherein the Narcissist twists everything around so that you are apologizing for *feeling wronged.*

If your guy or gal cannot seem to muster up an apology, even when clearly, undoubtedly in the wrong, you may be dealing with a Narcissist. Which means you will wait forever for your sweetie to make amends. If you stay with this kook, very soon you will stop expecting an apology and learn to keep your hurt feelings to yourself. Because your hurt feelings hurt the Narcissist's feelings, and how dare you be so inconsiderate? The Narcissist takes no prisoners in his or her righteous pursuit of "happiness." Are you ready to go down in the name of your sweetie's inflated ego?

What if I'm Not Sure?

If you're still confused, I don't blame you. You want to feel better, happier in your relationship, but you also want to give your sweetie the benefit of the doubt. After all, if Sweetie truly is a Narcissist, there is very little hope of improvement. Unless Sweetie's a teenager. In which case, put down this book and get your own therapy! Here are a few questions to answer before you throw in the towel:

- **Does Your Lover Have Over-the-Top Fantasies?**

Lofty goals are my favorite kind, and I think pipe dreams are the most fun. But some fantasies are so out there that they speak to extreme self-importance and probably were dreamt up by a Narcissist. We all love an underdog story, the horse that comes from behind to win the race, but this kook is so grandiose, it's aggravating.

Does your lover talk seriously about becoming President, a rock star, or a multi-millionaire? If he or she is on that track (degree, some cash, talent, an agent, etc.), that's one thing. But if Lover is still working at the Dairy Queen, you've got a problem. Fantasies could also have to do with possessions, experiences, and feelings. Listen to how your lover talks. Maybe he or she really isn't joking.

- **Does Your Sweetie Express Feelings of Envy?**

Again, we all get envious from time to time. We see something that someone else has, whether it is a hot car, a hot job, or a hot babe, and we want that for ourselves. But the Narcissist is actively envious. The Narcissist is obsessed with what others have and with the fact that he or she doesn't have it, too.

Does your sweetie talk frequently about other people's possessions, notice aspects of other people's lives that you don't, such as new clothing or jewelry, and then offer negative comments? Does your sweetie believe that others are also actively envying him or her? Pay attention. Take note. If Sweetie comments about other people frequently, Sweetie may be a Narcissist.

Very often, Narcissists are the best looking, most accomplished, charismatic people in the room. Their desire to be better than everyone else, to hear applause and receive attention, drives them to a level of success that others may find difficult to obtain. This kook wants you to succeed, too, and encourages you to do so. He or she makes suggestions about how you could improve your look, your career, and your relationships. This feels good. Your lover looks good. You look good together.

All of this makes it very hard to say, "No," to this kook. Once you get involved with one, extricating yourself is challenging at best. You rearranged your life to be with this person (because he or she expected it), and that means you might have to go back to being the person you were before (and you may not like that person very much).

Remember, falling in love with a Narcissist is a dangerous game. One that you will surely not win. If you are dating a Narcissist, get out and get out fast. More than that, get out clean. No loose ends and no opportunities for discussion. You're not strong enough for this. No one is.

The Neatnik

Julie said Stan was so obsessed with cleaning that he got up in the middle of the night to vacuum the carpet.

I have a hard time convincing some people that a Neatnik is a kook. Cleanliness, good hygiene, and organizational skills are attributes many of us – including me, and most parents of young children – aspire to have. Wives constantly complain about their cleaning-challenged husbands, and people who keep a clean home are held in high regard.

So what's so kooky about that? Nothing. Except when the cleaning takes over your life. Tidy is good. I love tidy. But the Neatnik's cleanliness is bordering on obsession. (If your partner does have an Obsessive Compulsive Disorder (OCD), you're partner is not a kook. OCD is a mental illness, not a character flaw. We'll cover this later in the chapter.)

When you think the living room is spotless, the Neatnik says it still requires hours of cleaning. When you're staying at a romantic hotel, the Neatnik makes the bed and cleans the room. When you bring home a puppy, the Neatnik makes you take it back because the dog will mess up the house. This kook is serious about sanitation, so much so that it becomes a barrier to fun, intimacy – life. But we'll get to that later, too.

Watching your every move, this kook makes it impossible for you to enjoy life. He's the guy who criticizes even the slightest speck of dirt. She's the gal who inspects the dishes after you've already washed them to her specifications. The Neatnik is the kook who washes towels after one use, scrubs the toilet daily, and can't go to sleep until everything is in its place.

While Neatniks are often the butt of jokes, being married to one is a lonely and demoralizing experience. You may think this is all about cleaning, that this kook just has some extreme habits and preferences, and that with a little help he or she could change. But you're wrong. This Neatnik has deep-seated issues that may never be solved, no matter how much you love and patience you have to give.

The Flexibility Factor

The American Heritage Dictionary defines a Neatnik as, "One who is habitually neat and orderly." Most of us at least try to develop a cleaning habit, and so we respect those who are disciplined enough to keep a neat and organized home. We don't see the downside of it, which is a lack of flexibility.

In any relationship, a little flexibility goes a long way toward fostering togetherness. When your guy is open to change and possibility, you can trust that he will make a place for you in his life. When your gal is willing to compromise a bit in order to satisfy both of your needs, you know that she values your opinion and cares about your own experience. It's no surprise that a Neatnik rarely gives in when it comes to cleanliness, but that behavior is also a sign that your guy or gal may not be flexible in other areas of life as well.

When your partner refuses to be flexible, it can be frustrating and cause hurt feelings. More than that, the lack of flexibility is a sign that your sweetie may not really want to be with you or anyone. Part of being in a relationship is learning from your partner, allowing your life to be influenced by him or her in a positive way. Relationships are designed to help us grow, expand, and obtain richer lives.

If your mate can't be flexible, there's a good chance that he or she doesn't really want a real relationship. Your mate may be attracted to you and enjoy your company, but does he or she *really* want to share a life with *you*? Or does your mate want some other version of you?

If your guy or gal has been rigid from the beginning, you have a problem. Remember, when we first start dating we have no problem calling in sick to stay in bed with our new lover, ignoring our sweetie's messy car, and letting dishes stay in the sink for two days because we're too busy making out. Eventually we resume our habits and manage to keep a clean house *and* be in love. But if you've been dealing with Neatnik behavior right off the bat, it's only going to get worse. Much, much worse.

Control Freaks in Training

We'll get into this more deeply later in the chapter, but Neatniks do what they do because they feel out of control. The constant effort to keep the kitchen floor so clean you could perform major surgery on it is the attempt of these kooks to restore order to their chaotic minds. On the whole, it's a harmless method for assuaging fears, but not all Neatniks stop there. Some evolve into Control Freaks.

If you haven't read the chapter yet, Control Freaks are dangerous kooks that chip away at your soul until you are left with virtually nothing that was once yours. Neatniks and Control Freaks frequently coexist in the same kook, though you may not meet the Dr. Jekyll side of your Mr. or Mrs. Hyde until well after you've settled into that darling Colonial. Neatniks require control over the condition of their homes, cars, and offices. This requires that tasks are done at the right time (whether it works for you or not), in the right manner (whether you agree or not), and at the right frequency (whether you think it's insane or not).

Do you see how a clean freak can become a control freak? Already you're adjusting your scheduling, habits, and opinions to suit the Neatnik. You think you're just placating your honey, trying to keep the peace in order to keep the relationship. But how long before you surrender completely? How long before you give up all of your autonomy in order to hang on to this kook? Neatnik to Control Freak is really not much of a stretch. It's important for you to realize that living with this kook very often means making room for another, more difficult kook. Are you really in the market for a package deal?

Gettin' Down and Gettin' Dirty

Are you thinking what I'm thinking? Good. I'm not the only one. Sex must drive this kook crazy! He or she probably has special requirements for sex, such as showering before – and after. The Neatnik isn't game for floor sex, bathroom sex, or any sex away from those clean sheets just put down for the occasion. Where's the fun in that?

When you deliberately take the fun and excitement out of having sex it's like digging a grave for your relationship. During difficult times, sex is often the glue that holds two people together. Why? Because sex with the one you love is a bonding experience, a way to express your feelings without words. Physical intimacy, unlike words, is rarely misinterpreted. The Neatnik's elaborate rules for "clean sex" get in the way of all that until it just isn't worth it anymore.

It may not be happening now, but eventually you will feel so self-conscious and restricted you'd rather give up than give in to bad sex. Sex isn't everything, but if your guy or gal makes real intimacy impossible, what do you have left?

Why Do Neatniks Do It?

As I mentioned earlier, true Neatniks indulge in obsessive cleaning in order to maintain order and control. When life gets stressful or chaotic, these kooks crank up the cleaning, hoping to gain a sense of calm amidst the turmoil. We all have our methods for dealing with extreme situations, but the Neatniks also carry this habit into everyday life. It's as if they are creating a super-clean bubble into which no harm can come. No crises, no disruptions, no bad news of any kind. And absolutely no changes.

The Neatniks fear change, especially when brought on by outside forces. They want to be in charge, and so change is threatening. Even the smallest shift disturbs the status quo and causes these kooks to feel overwhelmed. Time to organize the linen closet (for the seventy-seventh time), sterilize the sponges (bought just yesterday), and wash the ceiling (you're kidding, right?).

Of course, there is always a chance that your guy or gal is not a kook but has a treatable illness. When we think of obsessive cleaning, we automatically think of OCD. But OCD manifests itself as the compulsion to repeat tasks over and over, such as washing hands and locking doors.

Remember Jack Nicholson's character in the film *As Good As It Gets*? How he couldn't step on cracks in the sidewalk and had to order the same thing for lunch in the same restaurant every day? That's OCD. It's not Obsessive *Cleaning* Disorder; it's Obsessive Compulsive Disorder.

Neatniks may, however, have Obsessive Compulsive Personality Disorder (OCPD). OCPD manifests itself as inflexibility, rigidity, perfectionism, adherence to procedures, rules and systems, a strict moral code, and *excessive cleanliness and orderliness*. The mental health diagnostic "bible," the DSM-IV-TR, lists the following (abbreviated) traits of OCPD:

1. Dedication to work, prohibiting time for relationships.
2. Inflexibility, rigidity, and stubbornness.
3. Hoarding of money, also objects, regardless of value.

4. Insisting his or her ways, views, and methods are correct and possessing an inability to ask for help and delegate tasks.
5. Obsession with "details, rules, lists, order, organization, or schedules."
6. Perfectionism that is uncontrollable and detrimental to task completion.
7. Requiring adherence to a strict ethical and moral code (not related to religion or cultural background).

If your partner has four or more of these traits, and they interfere with his or her life, there's a good chance your partner has OCPD. Luckily, it can be treated. Contact a mental health professional for an official diagnosis and recommendations for treatment. Even if your Neatnik does *not* have OCPD, he or she still needs help in order to handle the normal ups and downs of life. Life is messy, and until the Neatnik accepts and learns to cope with this fact, the two of you will remain imprisoned by his or her kookiness.

Opposites Attract? (Or Why YOU Do It)

At first glance, the Neatnik seems like a good match for you-- clean, orderly, works hard, and has a strong ethical core that you admire. If you're not quite there yourself, the Neatnik appears to be exactly what you need to finally grow up and take life seriously. Besides, the Neatnik is dedicated and together enough to pick up your slack until you attain his or her level of perfection.

We get sucked into relationships with Neatniks in part because they seem to balance us out. You need your Neatnik, and your Neatnik needs you. Where one of you is strong, the other is weak. Where one of you is tough, the other is gentle. Where one of you is clueless, the other is skilled. Sounds great, doesn't it?

But if you are trying to balance your weaknesses and strengths with a Neatnik's weaknesses and strengths in order to form a perfect union, you've picked the wrong kook. The Neatnik can't balance anything because he or she has got only one thing on brain: A clean, well-ordered life to the exclusion of change, compromise, fun, relaxation and spontaneity. Yikes!

As I said in my first book, opposites may attract, but they stay together only if their values are in alignment. A concert pianist may fall in love with a professional wrestler in a match that seems doomed from the start. But if the pianist and the wrestler have similar values – such as family, or freedom, or privacy, or career – they could make it all the way to their golden anniversary.

You may admire the way your guy or gal takes care of things and cleans up after you, but do you really hold this value as dear as he or she does? Are you ready to sign up for a lifetime of rules and regulations just because your partner balances you out perfectly? Both of you are governed by your values. Can they coexist, or do you need to adopt the Neatnik's ways in order to keep the peace? The sad truth is the *only* way you can fit into the Neatnik's world is to give in to his or her demands. Are you prepared to do that...forever?

How to Spot the Neatnik

The first order of business is to stop reading this section and at least skim the Control Freak chapter to determine if your Neatnik is really a dangerous Control Freak in disguise. If you're (almost) certain that's not the case, you can move on to spotting the Neatnik kook.

The Neatniks can be hard to spot because it's common for them to hide the degree to which they're obsessed with cleaning and organization until after you're madly in love.

Some Neatniks are masters at hiding their kookiness until after the honeymoon, so it's important that you learn how to spot the signs.

- **Labels, Labels and More Labels**

The next time you're at your sweetie's place, take a look around. Is everything hyper-organized with labels for everything from spices to underwear? Do the closets hold storage bins neatly stacked with the contents clearly labeled? Does it seem like everything, literally *everything*, has a place and a label?

The Neatnik is a dedicated organizer. There are no junk drawers, no piles of papers, and no stacks of last year's magazines. The Neatnik can't abide by disorganization, and so when you investigate you will not find one single item out of place. He or she may even organize *your* stuff and criticize your home for its lack of perfect organization. Sound familiar?

- **Lists, Lists and More Lists**

The Neatnik loves to make lists. You'll find lists for everything, not just task lists or shopping lists. The Neatnik cleans out his or her car and makes a list of what was found there. The Neatnik makes lists of files deleted from his or her computer. The Neatnik lists the television shows to watch that week and when they will air. The Neatnik makes lists in order to think things through. The list makes your honey feel safe and secure; without it, he or she feels chaotic and out of control.

Does your guy or gal carry around a book of lists? Do you notice your sweetie keeping track of everything under the sun? Does he or she seem anxious when you suggest that you just "wing it" when shopping or traveling? If your sweetie is a list fanatic, there's a good chance your sweetie is also a Neatnik.

- **Rules, Rules and More Rules**

The Neatnik expects order in all aspects of life and so adheres to an elaborate system of rules. This kook is never in a quandary about what is right or wrong; he or she is right, and if you don't agree, you're wrong. A Neatnik doesn't seek the advice of friends because a Neatnik is never in doubt of what to do.

If your partner imposes a lot of rules on him or herself, you, or your relationship, you may have fallen for a Neatnik. Cleanliness and organization are just the outwardly visible signs of this kook, but they carry over into every aspect of his or her life. Excessive rules are a sign of inflexibility and the need for control, so go back and read the Control Freak chapter again. Are you sure your guy or gal isn't two kooks in one?

- **Scrubbing, Scrubbing, and More Scrubbing**

Like those bumper stickers that say, "I brake for _____" – fill in the blank: Chia Pets, garage sales, blondes – this kook brakes for dirt. Think back over the last month. How many times did your sweetie put off something in order to finish – or even start – cleaning something? Were you late because of it? Did you miss out on something, like dinner, a movie, or a make out session, because your sweetie was too preoccupied with a cleaning project?

If the world has to stop because your sweetie has the urge to clean up some dirt (real or imagined), you may be dating a Neatnik. Remember, these traits get only more extreme as your guy or gal gets more comfortable around you and your commitment to each other becomes stronger. Take his or her annoying cleaning habits and multiply them by ten – could you hack it long-term?

What if I'm Not Sure?

As I mentioned earlier, Neatniks routinely hide the breadth of their kookiness until after you've signed on the dotted line. If you suspect your sweetie is a Neatnik but you're not sure, these tips will help you scope him or her out:

- **Surprise Inspection**

Show up unannounced to find out if your darling really lives an orderly life when you're not around. It could be that he or she hired a cleaning crew to spiff up the place before your first at-home date. Or maybe Darling did it solo. The only way you can know for sure is to stop by without warning for a surprise inspection. You'll have to time it so that you arrive at least one week after your most recent visit so your guy or gal has had time to sufficiently mess up the place. You'll also have to find a way to get all the way into the place; just glancing over your sweetie's shoulder won't cut it.

- **Meet the Parents**

Meeting your honey's parents can tell you a lot about his or her unique kookiness. If you're serious enough to meet the parents, take a trip to Mom and Dad's place to investigate. Do the folks keep an exceptionally neat house? If so, this may be why your sweetie feels the need to do the same. But the reverse can be true as well.

If the folks are total pigs, your honey could be rebelling against his or her upbringing. But don't stop there. Look beyond the obvious, surface clues to find the truth. Is the house your sweetie grew up in chaotic or full of drama? Adopting a Neatnik persona may be his or her way of calming down after dealing with that stressful environment.

- **Stick to Your Guns**

If your house is clean enough, don't give in to your lover's demands for perfection. Once it starts, it could snowball. A non-kook might be annoyed but will get over it and just revert to complaining about your disgusting ways to his or her friends. A Neatnik could become very angry when you stick to your guns, and your rebelliousness may result in a breakdown or a breakup. But isn't it better to know if he or she loves you for you rather than your Dyson vacuum cleaner?

So what have you decided? Is your guy or gal a Neatnik kook? If the answer is, "Yes," I would like to offer you some hope. There is one type of person who can find harmony with a Neatnik, and that's another Neatnik. It is common to see yourself in the traits I list to help you spot the kooks. In this case, if you discover that you're a bit on the kooky side yourself, just get some ground rules down with your very own Neatnik and you'll probably live happily ever after. Because Neatniks love rules. Yours will probably even make a list of the rules so you can refer to them regularly. Two copies, in fact. One for each of you. Aww...isn't that sweet?

But if you're not even close to being a Neatnik, you're going to have to take a pass on this kook. I know, I know. Your life is orderly now. You can find things. You get things done. But the honeymoon won't last. Soon enough, this kook will berate you for your bad behavior – which is anything that doesn't follow his or her unique logic – and require strict obedience to the house rules of cleanliness and orderliness. Your life will be centered around keeping up with the mopping, cleaning, dishwashing, dusting, vacuuming, sterilizing, and other sexy tasks that *must* be done before life can move on.

Look, if you really need a clean house, just buy one. Hire a cleaning service, an organizational expert, a personal shopper, and a virtual assistant to keep your life shipshape and on track. Or look at it this way: A pristine house is highly overrated. It's certainly not worth enduring this kook's nonsense. Bye, bye Neatnik.

The Solo Artist

After seven blissful months, Annie said Todd still hadn't introduced her to his parents.

The Solo Artist is mysterious and frustrating. This kook makes you happy, treats you right, and seems just about perfect in nearly every way. Except for one, minor detail. You haven't met any of the important people in his or her life. No brunch with Mom and Dad. No cocktails with his coworkers after the company softball game. No long lunch with her best friend from college.

At first, you don't really mind it. After all, a hot new romance is supposed to be about just the two of you and all of the exciting things you can do with – and to – each other. The impromptu getaways, the long rambling walks, and entire weekends spent in virtual lockdown in your apartment.

But eventually, it's time to meet the folks. At some point, you're ready to show off your guy to your inner circle or bring your gal to the monthly all-family Sunday dinner. Your sweetie soon becomes your "...and guest" for every party, and you wait for him or her to reciprocate. But the Solo Artist never asks. No invitations. No impromptu meet-ups. Worse, the Solo Artist sidesteps the issue when you bring it up, so you're not even sure *why* he or she doesn't want you to meet the posse.

The natural evolution of romantic relationships requires meeting your sweetie's nearest and dearest. But for whatever reason, the Solo Artist has no interest in sharing his or her life with you. And that's the point, isn't it? The Solo Artist doesn't want to *share a life with you.* That's a significant problem, wouldn't you say? So if you've been hanging with a Solo Artist, be happy with what you've had. Because that's all you're going to get.

I Like Things the Way They Are...Almost

It's hard to argue when your seemingly perfect new lover says, "I like things the way they are," and, "I mean, don't you like it, too?" Of course you do. You just want more. You want the whole package, or you at least want to try for it. It's not that you don't love spending all of this time alone together, but you would *also* like to be treated as the *significant other*.

I use the word "significant" because that's how we want to feel as a relationship progresses. We are looking for milestones both little and big to help us feel secure, loved, and important. A key to his apartment. Her toothbrush in your medicine cabinet. Signing both of your names to his cousin's wedding present. Meeting her dad for a game of golf at the club.

These milestones also give us clues to future possibilities. If he invites you to his parents' summer home, it gives you permission to dream about having your wedding on their expansive lawn with the lake views. When she invites you to her office holiday party, you know there's a good chance you may be the one. You're more than just a fling. You're *significant*.

If you're both in it for the long haul, or at least entertaining the idea, you're going to have to spend time with *other people* eventually. So while you may be content with "the way things are," mark my words, one day it *will* piss you off. Because you want it all. And you deserve it. Unfortunately, the Solo Artist wants something different. To remain solo. On paper it sounds like a simple difference, but it's as complicated as it gets.

The Evolution of a Kook

The Solo Artist could actually be several kooks in disguise and could also transform from one kook to another. You see, in order to become a Solo Artist, one first has to be some other kook: A commitment-phobe, a loner, or perhaps something more diabolical like, say, a bigamist? There's a reason why your honey chose the life of a Solo Artist. What type of kook was your guy or gal *before* deciding to go solo?

A Solo Artist may continue to evolve into other kooks as well, may feel it necessary to adopt another kooky persona in order to maintain the Solo Artist lifestyle. Perhaps he or she would become a pathological liar, a manipulator, or something much worse, such as an abuser. Desperation can make people do things that go against their values. Kookiness can evolve into other, more severe kooky behavior.

Solo Artists could also be Control Freaks, keeping you in line by withholding parts of their lives. Or they could be Grifters who are keeping dirty little secrets. Or Buddies who really just see you as a friend with benefits. Or maybe even Loafers who don't want you to know the truth about their record-breaking sloth behavior.

It may be hard to imagine your sweetie pie in any of these roles, but if Sweetie Pie is a dyed-in-the-wool Solo Artist, you can bet he or she is more preoccupied with maintaining the status quo than maintaining a healthy, nurturing relationship with you.

Why Do Solo Artists Do It?

If you've fallen for a Solo Artist, you're dating a person who a) is ashamed of you and does not want to be seen slumming it with you, or b) is using you and never intends to make an honest woman/man out of you, or c) is also a cheater, the most common kook of all. No matter what the surface reason is, Solo Artists won't let anyone in, even you. And you know what? They never intended to.

When we date kooks, we always look for practical (i.e. fixable) reasons for why they do what they do. The Solo Artists may have a reasonable explanation for keeping you hidden from everyone else in their life, such as, "My family is really weird," or "I'm a sex symbol and can't be seen as taken." Okay. But is your Solo Artist willing to fix the problem or make a change?

I'm guessing the answer is, "No." Because the reason the Solo Artist goes it alone is deeper than that. This kook is not in love with you. Period. She doesn't want to live happily ever after by your side. Marrying you is the furthest thing from his mind. How do I know? Because when two people fall in love there is a natural desire to commingle their lives. You *want* to share your life with your sweetie. You *want* to introduce him to your friends, show her where you grew up, make your love part of your own beautiful life.

But you're alone in this desire. Solo Artists don't want to know you, *really* know you, because it means you might share a deeper connection, an emotional bond that is hard to sever when it comes time for this kook to move on. And the Solo Artist will most assuredly move on. Mark my words.

Don't You Want Me Baby? (Or Why YOU Do It)

One thing's for certain: You have a thing for un-gettable hotties. You like the thrill of the chase; you want to be the one who finally gets your guy or gal to submit and commit. You've got a serious conversion fantasy going -you know, the one wherein the mere sight of you can turn a player into a spouse in seconds flat? You think the Solo Artist just hasn't met the right person yet and that YOU are that person.

Maybe you didn't consciously go after your sweetie because he or she was a diehard Solo Artist, but something in you *knew* you weren't on stable ground. He's got you wondering if he really loves you. She has you strategizing your next move, hoping to win her heart. And my friend, some part of you likes it, needs it, or wants it.

Is there any chance YOU don't really want to commit? Are you pinning your hopes on a Solo Artist because some part of you isn't ready for a real, long-term relationship? Or are you attaching your happiness to a someday outcome because you really don't feel that great about the here and now? Ask yourself the hard questions and then answer them honestly. Otherwise you'll end up feeling like crap indefinitely, hoping your hottie finally wises up and lets you in.

Will the Solo Artist ever want to settle down? Possibly. But it won't be with you. If she's not giddy, wide-eyed, and ready to jump in now, she never will be. If he's not opening up, making plans, and including you in his daily life, he never will. You've got to be in love AND ready for love in order to do all that.

Whatever the reason behind your sweetie's solo act, it's time you come to terms with the fact that what you see is what you get. You can't make someone want you. Those are hard words to hear and even harder to accept, but that doesn't make them untrue. If your guy or gal is a Solo Artist, make a break for it and hold out for the real thing. You deserve it.

How to Spot the Solo Artist

Once you've been dating a Solo Artist for a few months, the signs are pretty obvious. You never get invited to family gatherings, work functions, or a night out with his or her pals. You haven't met any of your darling's friends or family, and Darling makes no effort to remedy that. You know all of this already, but there are some early signs that can help you spot this kook *before* you give your heart away.

- **Enough About Me, Let's Talk About You!**

In the beginning, when you stay up talking for hours, or close the restaurant filling each other in on the details of your lives, you can spot a Solo Artist if you really try. The Solo Artist rarely wants to talk about him or herself. Revealing names of friends and family just leads to more questions and eventually to questions like, "When can I meet them?" As soon as you ask about your Solo Artist's life, he or she steers the conversation back to you and hangs on every word you say.

It's tough to peg a Solo Artist when he or she is listening attentively to your story about playing the part of "The Scarecrow" in the third grade. No one ever seemed to care about the fact that you won the statewide spelling bee three times in a row, and it's a bit intoxicating to have someone want to hear that story – any story – all the way through. But if you can set your own ego aside, you might be able to do it. Spot the kook, that is.

- **Let's Go to Your Place**

The Solo Artist loves to spend time at your place and rarely asks you to spend the night at his or her abode. Sure, you've seen your sweetie's pad, but she's probably just "picking up a few things" and heading back to your place. Before you think it's sweet of your new guy to add fifty minutes to his commute just so you can wake up in your own bed, ask yourself why you never watch a movie at his place?

I'll tell you why. Because that would mean you would have to shop for groceries nearby or pick up a pizza down the street. You might run into someone your cupcake knows. Or one of Cupcake's pals may stop by unannounced, and then Cupcake would be forced to introduce you. It's much safer for the Solo Artist to camp out at your place, and that's the real reason why he or she stays over all of the time – no matter how many times your own personal Solo Artist tells you your place "just feels more like home."

- **All New Haunts**

Likewise, the Solo Artist isn't interested in taking you to a favorite coffee shop or any other place he or she likes to hang out. You're not going to drive to his college watering hole or meet her for lunch near the office. Instead, the Solo Artist will make sure you have all new haunts. Special places. *Your* places. Remember how you want to be significant? Hard to argue with that now, isn't it?

- **Solo PDA**

I'm not talking about public displays of affection; I'm referring to your sweetie's handheld. Whether it's a Blackberry or iPhone, the Solo Artist isn't sharing. There aren't going to be any moments of you two huddling together to compare schedules because this kook doesn't want you to know about his nephew's upcoming Bar Mitzvah or her best friend's graduation party. The Solo Artist keeps his or her PDA close to the vest and probably doesn't take it out much, either. This may seem like a breath of fresh air in our technology-obsessed culture, but if you've hooked up with a Solo Artist, it's really because he or she doesn't want to share.

What if I'm Not Sure?

Are you *really* still wondering if your guy or gal is a Solo Artist? Because the signs are pretty black and white. Okay. So you're hanging on because you really like this one. Here's what you might try if you're not sure you're knoodling with a Solo Artist:

- **Stop By**

If you really want to know if you're dating a Solo Artist, just take the initiative. Stop by the office and invite your honey to lunch. Be "in the neighborhood" when you're not scheduled to hang out. You'll be able to tell how Honey really feels about you from the reaction to your spontaneous visit.

Two words of caution: Don't. Stalk. Don't stop by unannounced several times a week, or you may scare away a perfectly good mate who just happens to be waiting for the right time to introduce you to his or her motley crew of pals and loved ones. In other words, don't let *your own* kookiness scare away a great date.

- **Invite Your Sweetie In**

Sometimes, the best way to let someone know what you want is to give it before you get it. Invite your muffin to important and random events in your own life, and let Muffin know you are looking forward to the day he or she will do the same. If you are lucky enough to just have a shy one on your hands, Muffin may just be waiting for you to make the first move.

Again, the Solo Artist is a head-trip because this kook could have any number of reasons why he or she wants to go it alone. Don't let solving the mystery sidetrack you from the task at hand -- determining if you are dating a Solo Artist. The "why" doesn't really matter because you're not going to fix it no matter how patient you are or how hard you try.

If it turns out you are in love with a Solo Artist, your best bet is to give that dreaded ultimatum. Either let me into your life or let me go. You're not asking for blood tests and a three-bedroom Colonial. You just want to know the real him or her. You want to be a part of your sweetie's life. You want to be...*significant*.

If it turns out that you're not, what's the point?

The Threesome

Emily said Ryan's best friend hung around so much that she felt like she was dating both of them.

Dating a Threesome can seem like a good bargain – after all, you get two for the price of one. But do you really *need* two? More often than not, a Threesome kook brings nothing but trouble; double trouble, that is. It's like that trough of ketchup you bought at the wholesale liquidators. It seemed like a great deal when you paid for it, but it didn't take long for you to resent the giant ketchup container for the space it consumed in your refrigerator.

The Threesome rarely seems like a kook when you first hook up. You like the fact that your pumpkin has a loyal friend; you may even really like the friend and see it as a bonus of dating the Threesome. Besides, you'd rather Pumpkin hang out with a friend instead of a potential love interest. These are just some of the rationalizations you run through as you disregard the signs that there is a kook in the house. Blinded by love, you ignore the fact that your guy lets his best friend come over unannounced at any time of day, which he frequently does at 3:00 a.m. Lost in Lovesick Land, you conveniently forget that your gal left in the middle of your hot date in order to console her best friend after a bad breakup – or a bad hangnail.

The Threesome is the kook who can't go one day without talking to his or her pal. She's the gal who always takes her friend's calls, even during moments of passion. He's the guy who routinely buys three tickets to events so his friend can come along. The Threesome is the kook who makes his or her friend the priority over you and won't hesitate to drop everything – even you – to be with that friend.

It's natural for single guys and gals to have close friendships. But once true love walks in the door, those friendships must change in order to make room for the new relationship. You may think that your darling will eventually adjust his or her social life to include more of you and less of his or her best chum, but don't count on it. If your sweetie is a Threesome brand of kook, you can look forward to a long courtship – just you and your sweetie...and the best friend. Congratulations!

Bosom Buddies

When you date a Threesome, you get a new lover *and* a new best friend, only not in the same person. The assumption is that you will automatically like your new sweetie's bosom buddy as much as Sweetie does and welcome him or her into your life just as your sweetie did. In fact, you should feel honored to be included in this tight, loyal friendship. They don't let just *anyone* in.

Sooner rather than later, you are expected to share your feelings with not one but two people or at least accept the fact that your honey will automatically tell Best Friend everything you say. Worse, Best Friend will offer up his or her *valued* opinion in response, and none of this will be shared with you. You're expected to become best friends with your sweetie's best friend and then understand when they exclude you from the conversation. It's like high school all over again.

Thick as thieves, your sweetie and his or her pal also have secrets they will never reveal to you, and some of them are about you! But perhaps the most annoying facet of dating a Threesome is the knowledge that your dearest doesn't think twice about airing your dirty laundry in front of his or her best, and most trusted, friend – despite the fact that you've only just met.

The trouble with the Threesome is this kook just can't seem to live without his or her best friend. The Threesome holds the BFF in such high regard that your opinion is worthy only of secondary consideration. Your honey may ask you for advice, even lean on you for comfort, but in the end, it's the best friend who gets the last word on everything and everyone. Even you.

Three's a Crowd

When you read this headline, you probably figured you could skip over this section. After all, you already *know* that three is a crowd; that's obvious. Well, did you know that I was talking about *you*, not the best friend? Not what you expected, right? You might want to read this section after all.

It's true that your lover includes the best friend in almost all of your plans. Even those that were meant to be private or romantic somehow become a group activity. So for you, three is most definitely a crowd, and you want this pal to get a partner, get a second job...get a life, so you can get on with yours. But that isn't going to happen anytime soon. Because the hard truth is *you're* the one who's crowding this duo. That's what makes this kook so kooky.

Close friends operate as one unit. They have their own habits, rituals, and commitments. If your guy or gal is a die-hard Threesome, these aspects of their friendship are cemented in stone. When you enter into a relationship with one of them, they both feel uncomfortable. Despite the fact that your honey seems into you and tells you so, his or her routine is disturbed. Honey has to make adjustments to accommodate you *and* the best friend, and if Honey's a genuine Threesome, your relationship won't last. Eventually, this kook will have to choose his or her friend over you in order to maintain the friendship. Three's a crowd, my friend. And you're the one who is crowding this well-established couple. Makes you feel a little sick to your stomach, doesn't it?

Breaking Up the Dynamic Duo

Before you can officially nab this kook, you first have to break up the buddies. There's just no room for you as long as your sweetie's best friend is providing most – or all – of the emotional support he or she needs. When all you have is sex and occasional companionship, there cannot be real intimacy between you, and there certainly cannot be true love. Sweetie may really like you, but as long as Sweetie and Best Friend are still joined at the hip, you're not getting anywhere with this kook.

Likewise, don't expect to get what *you* need emotionally from the Threesome. Your darling is giving all of his or her good advice and comforting thoughts away to the pal of pals. By the time you get to log some time with Darling, you get the dregs. The leftovers. The scraps. Since the best friend is using up all the good stuff, the only course of action is to break up this dynamic duo once and for all.

Don't get me wrong; I'm not advocating busting up a healthy, loving friendship. What I *am* suggesting is the other two individuals in your Threesome have blurred the lines of friendship to the exclusion of others, namely you. You don't have to orchestrate a major falling out; you just have to get them both to agree to set some boundaries and make you and your relationship with your sweetie a priority. A *sacred* priority.

You heard me. You have to get them both to agree. And so the sad truth comes out. It isn't going to happen. Remember, your sweetie is not a normal person with the ability to hear reason and act on it. Your Sweetie's a kook, which by definition makes him or her unpredictable, irrational, unreliable, and frustrating beyond belief. Nope. You're SOL, my friend.

Why Do Threesomes Do It?

Like the Buddy, the Loafer, and the Lost kooks, the Threesome doesn't really want to grow up. The best friend serves as a buffer to help your sweetie avoid commitment. As long as your Threesome has his or her comrade close by, there will be no marriage, no kids, and no responsibilities of any kind. Oh, he or she may pay lip service to wanting everything you want, but this kook has had an exit strategy from day one.

Could it be that your guy or gal just isn't as into you as you thought? Sure. But it could also be that your honey just wants to have it all -- you *and* freedom. Enter the best friend. The best friend takes up so much space, you never have a chance to get close enough to this kook, and eventually, you go on your merry way in search of saner pastures. See how well that works?

Of course, there is always the possibility that your lover and the best friend are just a little too close for comfort. Does someone in this Threesome love someone else just a little *too much*? Hey, it could happen. Jerry Springer guests aside, friendship often leads to deeper feelings of romantic love, and society does not allow these relationships to bloom naturally without repercussions.

It could be that your guy or gal is in love with his or her best friend, or vice versa, or both, and just can't admit it yet. This scenario is not as rare as you think, so observe. Spotting the signs of romantic love is much easier than spotting the kook. Besides, if you do see love disguised as friendship, you don't really have to spot the kook, do you?

Three's Company (or Why YOU Do It)

Remember the hit show from the 70s and 80s, *Three's Company*? If you're too young to remember it on the air, perhaps you caught it in reruns or at least watched the show's *True Hollywood Story* on E! Entertainment Television. In case you're clueless about the plot, the show was about two women and one man who lived in the same apartment. At the time the show aired, this was considered taboo because all of the roommates were single.

Three's Company ran for years and often centered on how one roommate got in the way of another roommate's dating adventures. The roommates changed, but everyone stayed single until the very end of the run. Why? Because the show wouldn't be any good if even one of them settled down. The characters rarely had steady boyfriends or girlfriends because that would have upset the delicate balance.

If you're involved with a Threesome kook, there's a good chance that you don't really want to settle down, either. You're happy with being single. You like the sitcom that is your life, and though you may give lip service to marriage, kids, and the whole shebang, you really aren't ready for it any more than the Threesome is. Just like Chrissy, Jack, and

Janet, you'd rather play the field for a bit longer. In other words, you want your program to stay on the air for a while. Why not? It's a good show.

How to Spot the Threesome

Like an extra head or a man in a gorilla suit, the Threesome is about as obvious as it gets – once you start dating. Because just about the time you expect the best friend to step aside a few nights a week, he or she doesn't. Here are a few signs that your guy or gal may be a Threesome:

- **Has No Boundaries**

The Threesome kook operates no differently when dating than when not dating. His or her BFF can come over any time, night or day, with or without warning. It could be weeks, even months before you and your honey go on a date without his or her appendage, and that's only because the friend went out of town.

It's easy to deal with your sweetie's close pal if there are firm boundaries in place. In non-Threesome relationships, friends respect the time needed to pursue romantic relationships. In fact, it is entirely normal for friends to get the shaft during the hot and heavy first weeks of new love. If your lover can't seem to ditch the best friend to spend quality time with you and doesn't really seem to want to, I would bet he or she's a Threesome. Expect joint vacations and dorky comments about being the Three Musketeers. If it sounds childish, it's because it *is* childish. Establishing healthy boundaries in all of our relationships is a sign of growth and maturity. But your guy or gal doesn't want to grow up, remember?

- **Puts Friends First**

In the film *Save the Last Dance*, the hero punches his childhood friend in defense of his new girlfriend. Later, after the hero and his girl have a falling out, he apologizes to his friend, saying, "Blood's thicker than blondes," referring to the fact that they were "blood brothers." In Shakespeare's tragic play *Othello*, the title character betrays his lover because he chose to believe his evil, manipulative "friend" over her. In fact, Othello didn't even *ask* Desdemona if Iago's accusations were correct – he just got right down to killing her and only then realized his mistake.

The Threesome kook is never going to choose you over the best pal no matter what catastrophes you orchestrate to test his or her devotion to you. Your darling has his or her friend at the top of the list, and until they "break up," you'll never move up. This kook will always side with his or her friend over you. It's pretty much a lose-lose situation, don't you think?

- **Can't Keep His or Her Own Counsel**

Before the Threesome can make a move, this kook must first consult with the other half. By now you've figured out that that's not you. This kook is so used to asking the pal for advice that he or she never even considers going it alone, much less asking someone else – like, say, you, the supposed lover – for advice.

It's easy to spot this behavior as your guy or gal will remain in near constant contact with his or her best friend. They will use the phone, email, and texting to stay in touch. This duo keeps tabs on each other like a mother keeps track of her children. They know each other's work schedules, favorite haunts, and probably their next thought. At first it may seem cute (really?), or endearing (that's pushing it), but it doesn't take long for this childish (here we go again) behavior to grate on your nerves. Fortunately, it's just irritating enough to help you spot this kook. See? There's an upside to everything.

What if I'm Not Sure?

Is there a chance that your dreamboat will shed his or her shadow and sign up with you? Maybe, if he or she's not a Threesome kook. If you're still not sure and would like to find out, may I first offer a few words of caution? Be extremely careful when getting between close friends. Bosom buddies are fiercely loyal, and you may end up losing your lover in your pursuit of a romantic weekend alone. Above all else, don't diss the best friend. Ever. Here are a few ideas to help you test the waters safely (try them all, not just one):

- **Take it Down a Notch**

As I suggested earlier, there's a good chance that neither of you are ready to get serious. Something about this person says "unavailable" because of his or her attachment to the best friend, and some part of you was attracted to that.

So take it down a notch. Keep it casual, fun, and light. Set your worry and concerns aside, and enjoy the time you have together.

If Best Friend's tolerable, try to get to know him or her and get on his or her good side. You may come to understand why your honey is so attached to this person and feel more relaxed about the whole situation. If you slow things down, a Threesome will be happy with the status quo, but a non-kook will eventually ask to speed things up. It's a safe way to find out which one you're dating and protect your heart in the process.

- **Set Up Your Own Boundaries**

No matter if you're dating a Threesome or a person who just enjoys having a good time with his or her best friend, it's fair to ask for a few boundaries. You're entitled to at least one date night a week with just you and your sweetie. And that getaway you've been planning? That's for just the two of you as well, no matter if the best friend was counting on going or not. You may also request that the best friend stay away when you're spending the night or not call past a certain hour. Whatever boundaries you need, set them up. A non-kook will rise to the occasion, and a Threesome will tattle to his or her friend and then call it quits. Better you find out now rather than end up living with both of them!

- **Double Date**

Who says you have to exclude your sweetie's best friend from all of your fun? Show you care and that you want him or her to be part of things by setting the best friend up with one of your cute, available pals. Suggest a double date, one wherein the four of you can have a ball but your little matchmaking guinea pigs can still have an opportunity to get to know each other. If it works out, you may even turn this Threesome into a Foursome, and there's nothin' kooky about that! (Get your mind out of the gutter, would ya?)

If your sweetheart is a non-kook who wants to make things work with you, he or she will probably be thrilled at the prospect of the best friend finding a new love. The stress of spending time with both of you may be getting to your sweetie, and you, being the genius you are, have given your guy or gal the perfect out. If it's a good match, you'll be on good terms with the best friend forever. If your guy or gal is a Threesome, the idea simply won't fly. Easy enough.

The Threesome is a kook who cares about his or her peeps and takes great pains to help them. Admirable qualities in a mate, but not when the mate won't – or can't – make room for you. It's pretty darn kooky to have a friend who is so up in your business that he or she can talk in detail about your sex life, knows which one of you won the fight, and can decode your secret language. It's even kookier when your guy or gal accepts this behavior as the norm and does nothing to make you feel special, wanted, and important.

Relationships require privacy, especially in the beginning. Heck, even polygamists allow the husband to spend time getting to know the future sister wife before she is welcomed into the fold. No matter how well you reason, how loud you rant, and how long you cry, you will never get the Threesome to see the light. You're better off letting your sweetie and his or her sidekick ride off into the sunset without you. You were just passing through anyway.

The Unavailable

Mary said that Todd still celebrated Christmas with his ex.

The UnAvailable is the guy or gal who poses as available but really isn't. I'm not talking about liars and cheats – that's another type of kook entirely. I'm referring to the person who seems to be available until you scratch beneath the single surface to find that he or she is still attached to the ex in some extreme fashion.

The UnAvailables may not even know how attached to their exes they really are; he may not see a problem with storing his boat in her garage, and she doesn't understand what the big deal is over her picking up a birthday present for his mom. After all, they don't live together anymore (well, as soon as the lease is up), they have separate bank accounts (oh, yeah, we forgot to do that), and they don't have sex anymore (ummm...what exactly do you mean by *sex?*).

UnAvailables are the kooks who masquerade as available when they still have their exes on speed dial. He's the guy who lives in his own nondescript apartment but stores most of his personal belongings in his ex wife's garage. She's gal who still calls her ex boyfriend for advice (in fact, he's the *first* person she calls when she's in trouble). He's the guy who texts inside jokes to his ex; she's the gal who still shows up at all of the ex's family functions.

We all know relationships don't necessarily end just because the judge signs the papers. It's tough to break free from the one you promised to love forever and ever. Really tough. Severing ties emotionally is even more difficult and often impossible. So even though your sweetie claims to be completely over the ex, it might not be true. He or she may still want to spend time with the ex, may still need something the ex has to offer, or worse: Your guy or gal could actually still love the ex.

The sad fact is that the UnAvailable can never be yours. Yup. Not ever. It doesn't matter how gorgeous you are, how much money you have, or how understanding and patient you are. Even if you're a superstar in the bedroom, you can't make an UnAvailable available. That's an inside job, and as long as you're hanging around, your lover can never have the space to get the closure he or she needs to move on.

But I'm the Love of My Darling's Life!

Remember that scene in *Casablanca* wherein Humphrey Bogart is standing in the rain on a train platform in Paris, reading Ingrid Bergman's farewell letter as the ink runs off the page? She's supposed to meet him there, and together they will escape Paris before the Nazi occupation. Great stuff, right? I've got news for you: That's you standing in the rain. That's *your* "Dear Rick" letter, *your* anguish, *your* shock and disappointment.

Granted, Ilsa thought her husband was dead when she fell in mad passionate love with Rick. But once she realized her former flame was still alive, it was "So long, Rick," and, "Hello, Hubby." Sure, her husband was the leader of the Nazi resistance movement, but hey, Rick was hot. Okay, maybe not cute, but handsome in a dark and brooding kind of way. Anyway, Rick was her real, grown-up love, and she broke his heart – and her own – because she couldn't betray her ex.

It just goes to show you, it's not over 'til it's over – even if the ex is dead! You may be thinking, "Come on, Adryenn, that's an extreme example." Maybe. But the point isn't *why* Ilsa went back to her husband or even that her husband came back from the dead. The point is that she still felt a sense of loyalty to him, and that loyalty was strong. Stronger than great sex, great times, and even great love. Ilsa was Rick's UnAvailable, and we all know, as we watch him walk off into the sunset, that his heart will never recover. How will your heart fare?

But My Lover Is a Really _ _ _ _ _ _ _ _ _!

Fill in the blank: Nice guy. Great gal. Sweet man. Lovely woman. Gentle soul. Pure Spirit. I'm sure you're 100% right. The UnAvailable is rarely malicious, just lost, or confused, or maybe even delusional. Again, this person is not the one who is maliciously keeping a big kahuna of a secret that will surely bust your heart wide open. This is the person who really doesn't see anything wrong with what he or she is doing.

The UnAvailable generally doesn't withhold the little facts that, like tracks in the forest, will lead you to the truth. Those seep out slowly. The more time you spend with your UnAvailable, the more you learn about his or her attachment to the ex. The vacation home they still co-own. The roses he sends her on their anniversary, *for sentimental reasons*. The honeymoon photos she displays proudly.

But your cupcake is a great date, a sweet lover, and a compassionate soul. There's nothing to worry about. It's nice that Cupcake still cares about the ex. You would want that if you ever broke up, right? (Keep talking until it sounds believable or just plain silly...which it is!)

It's Not Sweetie's Fault, It's the Ex!

Blaming your lover's ex is *the* most common bad habit among second (or third or fourth) loves. In my book *Every Single Girl's Guide to her Future Husband's Last Divorce*, I devoted an entire chapter to learning how to deal with the ex wife in a positive way. In my experience, letting your guy or gal off the hook and channeling your energy into hating the ex is the worst mistake you can make. Why? Because it takes the focus off of your partner and places it firmly on the ex, leaving you vulnerable to deception, whether or not that deception is intentional.

Do you feel his or her ex is inappropriate, crosses the line, and maybe still wants your lover back? It could be true. But is that about the ex, or is that about your one and only? Until you take the focus off of the ex, you won't know for sure.

Look, your guy can make up his own mind; your gal is perfectly capable of cutting ties. It really does take two to tango, so don't let your sweetie off so easily. The truth is a divorce leaves a lot in its wake, and scads of unresolved emotional, logistical, and financial issues may float in with the tide from time to time. This doesn't mean the ex is out for blood – or a reunion. If you're dating someone who is just coming off of a big bad breakup, you're going to have stuff. If you want a baggage-free date, find yourself a nubile virgin and get down to business. (What? It's sarcasm. Geez!)

Why Do UnAvailables Do It?

If you've ever ended it with a serious love, you know it's rarely a clean break. Love lingers long after you decide to split, not to mention the financial, emotional, and physical entanglements that have to be, well, untangled. The UnAvailable may have a problem navigating all of this rocky terrain and, until meeting you, really didn't feel motivated to try very hard.

Your guy or gal may not have tied up all of the loose ends simply because old habits are hard to break. The ex is familiar, and even though they would rather walk on glass then spend time together, even the fights offer a sense of normalcy in a sea of brand new everything. Or, your sweetie may hang around the ex out of a need to control him or her, which means you probably have a double-kook on your hands.

There are also a host of financial and other practical reasons why two people would stay connected in unhealthy ways long after they break up. For example, a shared apartment lease can keep a severed couple in the same apartment for months. But is it *really true* that your guy or gal can't get out of it? Maybe, maybe not.

The truth is if your sweetie is an UnAvailable, he or she hasn't really left the previous relationship, and there's a good chance Sweetie will end up with reuniting with the ex. Some part of the UnAvailable is not ready to completely douse the "old" flame, and until your sweetie can douse it for good, he or she can't move on with you.

Breaking Up is Hard to Do (or Why YOU Do It?)

The UnAvailable lover is hard to break up with because, like it or not, we all get caught up in the human soap opera. Yes, the *fact* that your sweetheart is still enmeshed with the ex actually *keeps you* in the relationship. All of that unfinished business has an allure. If you're objecting out loud right now, let me ask you a few questions:

- Do you think about your sweetie's ex? Do you look at his or her picture and wonder about their "happy days." How often?
- Do you ever compare yourself to the ex? Do you think, "Would she wear this?" or "Was he better than me in the sack?"
- Do you discuss the ex with your guy or gal? Do you have heated discussions? Do you present demands, fly off the handle, or in general have any drama *in your own* relationship about his or her ex?

- Do you know WAY TOO MUCH about the ex (i.e. could you correctly answer a final *Jeopardy* question about the ex?)?

If you answered "yes" at least twice, you may have a problem, and it goes way beyond being involved with an UnAvailable. If you're attracted to this type of mate, breaking up with him or her is just making room for the next one. You might as well get your *Martha Stewart* label maker out, clear out a sock drawer, and permanently label it, "For My Darling UnAvailable."

Human beings are drawn to drama and conflict. We can't help looking at the car accident by the side of the road (they even had to give the phenomenon its own name—rubbernecking), or the 12,000 television updates about another movie star in rehab. It doesn't matter who we are -- male or female, gay or straight, truck driver or graphic designer. We all turn up the volume for the catfights, the heartfelt declarations of love, and the closing arguments. Why? Because we have to see what happens. Translation: We have to see who wins.

Your involvement with an UnAvailable may feed your own urge for drama to whatever degree it is present in you.

Some of us cringe at the thought of it in our own lives, but others thrive on the real-life emotional tug-of-war a still-present ex can create in our relationship.

Likewise, you may get off on the competitive aspect of it. If you're in it to win it, having the ex around is actually a turn on because it raises the stakes. You didn't just nab the lover of your dreams; you broke the hold the ex had on him or her AND erased all memory of the ex from the heart and brain. You won, and you won BIG.

See what I mean? If you get anything out of being involved with an UnAvailable, breaking up may not only be hard, it might even be impossible. (Do you think that might be why the ex is still hanging around...?)

How to Spot the UnAvailable

UnAvailable kooks are pretty easy to spot, though maybe not at first. In the beginning of the relationship, when you are both still giving each other space (or playing hard to get), you might not notice the signs. Once you're at the stage wherein you're keeping tabs on each other, seeing each other every other day and texting sweet nothings every few hours, the signs will be like giant billboards in the sky.

Remember, the UnAvailable usually doesn't see anything *wrong* with his or her involvement with the ex. Hence, the signs are right out there in the open. But don't worry. If you can't spot 'em, your friends will pick them out right away. If you're lucky, they'll even schedule an intervention on your behalf. Until then, here are some basic signs to help you spot the UnAvailable:

- **No Forwarding Address**

If your honey is still living with the ex, no matter how logical the explanation is, you have an UnAvailable. Even if Honey sleeps in the guest room, in the basement, or in the shed out back, they are still *living together*. Sharing living space blurs the lines of any relationship; even roommates get too involved with each other's lives. And when you're shacked up with the ex, those boundary lines are virtually nonexistent.

"But my sweetie has his (or her) own apartment, Adryenn." Okay. Let's talk about that apartment. Take a look around. Does your guy or gal get mail forwarded from the old place or is there very little mail with no forwarding address label? What about his stuff? Does the apartment feel homey and lived in or sort of empty? Does it reflect her personality through keepsakes, closets full of clothes, books, and other items?

If you've hooked up with an UnAvailable, it's likely that your sweetie doesn't spend a lot of time in the new space perfect for singles. Or Sweetie may still have all of his or her stuff at the old place, which really makes the new place a long-term hotel room. We all need time to get our life back together after a breakup, but there should be evidence in the home that your guy or gal is making an effort to move on. I'm talking groceries, plants, some new items picked up at Pottery Barn or Home Depot, and, especially, pieces of mail with that telltale yellow forwarding sticker.

- **The "Honey Do" List**

When your guy or gal still has a to-do list from the ex, you're probably dating an UnAvailable. Think about it. What is the *first* thing you want to stop doing when you officially break up with someone? All of the crap the ex made you do when you were still together! Fix the toilet, pick up the dry cleaning, drive Mother to bingo. That list of chores and responsibilities is par for the course in any serious relationship, but your guy or gal should NOT be checking off tasks for his or her ex.

A "honey do" list, whether it is long, short, recent, or still to come, is really about availability -- your lover making him or herself available to the ex. He agrees to go with her to negotiate a deal on a new car. She has no problem wrapping Christmas presents for his nieces and nephews. He leaves *your* bed to, well, fill in the blank (fix her plumbing, protect her from her new nasty boyfriend, etc.). She meets him for lunch to help him debrief after therapy.

Whatever the task, your guy or gal shouldn't be running off to the ex for every little bump in the night. If it pertains to their children, of course he or she has to attend to their needs. But if your darling is still running errands and solving problems for his or her ex, you may want to rethink that ride off into the sunset.

- **Best Friends**

Beware of people who claim their ex is their best friend. I get that it's hard to break ties with a great love, especially if they were friends first, but once they call it quits, it's time for a new bosom buddy. If your guy or gal has an active, close friendship with the ex, it means at least some of his or her emotional needs are being met by the former flame. It also means they do things alone together, things that resemble dates. And it means they share confidence and generally rely on each other for support and guidance. Which, again, sounds like dating.

The exception is if your sweetheart has kids in common with his best-friend-ex-spouse/lover/fling, then they obviously have more reason to spend time together, and they most certainly should strive to be on *friendly* terms with each other. In fact, research has shown that children whose divorced parents are openly friendly have fewer problems than parents who only discuss report cards. Add that to the fact that they will be tied together forever through the children, don't expect that cord to get without serious consequences for the kiddo(s)!

If your sweetie doesn't want to give up his or her friend and still wants to be with you, suggest a compromise. If you can stomach it, spend time as a group, or go on a double date. Remember, if you agree to this, you will have to be the picture of calm. No snotty comments or steely stares. If your guy or gal recoils at the thought of sharing the ex with you (or vice versa), they were probably made for each other and you're just a tiny chapter in their own book of love.

What if I'm Not Sure?

It is possible that your dumpling is simply lazy and just hasn't gotten around to severing ties with the ex. If you're not sure if Dumpling is an UnAvailable, try asking him or her these two questions:

- **Where Do You See Us In _ _ _ _ _ Years?**

Okay, this is a tough question that could open up a giant can of worms, but inquiring minds want to know. Is your sweetie for real or just playing house? Does your guy want to start fresh with you or is he just biding his time until his ex realizes the errors of her dumping ways? Is your gal thinking long-term or is she saving her heart for the one that got away?

When the time is right, ask your sweetie about his or her vision for the future. More importantly, ask if you're in it. While neither of you may be ready for joint tenancy and baby names, knowing that your guy or gal wants to love you longer than next Tuesday is a good sign. If, on the other hand, your sweetie can't even *talk* about the future, much less plan for the future, you may be dealing with an UnAvailable.

- **How Over is "Over?"**

Find out if your guy or gal is truly available by asking about the warning signs you've spotted so far. Is it really over between the two of you? How over, exactly? Did you close your joint checking account? Are you still co-owners on the house? How often do you talk on the phone, email each other, or get together? What about the stuff? Have you separated your books, furniture, and dishes? What about the old circle of friends or the relatives of the ex? Are you still in contact with them?

You know your sweetie, so you know which questions to ask. The point of this exercise is to find out if your guy or gal is ready to move on with you, or is stuck in the past. After a few questions, you should have a pretty good idea of where they are, and where they can (or can't) ever be.

- **Would You Be Willing to Cut Ties?**

Now that you know about all of the entanglements, ask your honey if he or she would be willing to close the book on the old flame. It's a fair question, considering Honey's involved with you and may or may not have made certain promises or pronouncements about your future together. Until your ex cleans up these loose ends, there will be no room in his or her life – or heart – for you.

Be brave. Ask. If you're nervous about it, I think you already know the answer. But you probably knew the truth when you started reading this chapter, didn't you?

No doubt, it's a major bummer when you realize your single guy or gal really has a lock on his or her heart. While there may be conniving UnAvailable kooks, most are mainly just people who cannot move on. They may want to. They may need to. But something keeps the UnAvailable hanging on, and it's that "something" that stands in the way of your future happiness.

If you have fallen for an UnAvailable, it's time to go on hiatus. Notice how I didn't say "cut and run?" Set your UnAvailable free to take care of business, get some therapy, and buy some furniture. But leave the door open for your sweetie to walk back into your life, 100% available and ready for action. This does not mean that you will wait patiently for that day to come – because it might never come – but it does offer both of you an opportunity to get on with things, knowing there is a glimmer of hope for your own budding love.

THE 12-STEPPER

Janine said Rob was so consumed by his recovery that he refused to take a honeymoon for fear of being away from his support group.

Before we dive in to spotting this kook, let me make myself perfectly clear: I am not dissing Alcoholics Anonymous or any other recovery program. Twelve-step groups have helped millions of people face their addictions and live happy, substance-free lives. So if your guy or gal is living a healthy life and just happens to attend 12-step meetings or some other support group in order to *stay healthy*, that is NOT kooky.

So what *is* a 12-Stepper? This is the kook who has built a life around recovering from something or another, be it drugs, alcohol, sex, food, gambling, shopping, a bad divorce, bankruptcy, or even just a lonely childhood. And that recovery is the all-consuming center of the 12-Stepper's life.

Everything and everyone takes a back seat to this kook's healing process. Including you.

She's the gal who won't date anyone until her sponsor gives the thumbs up. He's the guy who meets his children-of-divorce support group every night after work. These are the kooks who can't make a move without discussing it with "the group," who have only sober friends, and who expect you to schedule your life around their recovery. The 12-Steppers treat you as though you couldn't possibly understand and yet never include you in the healing process or invite you to group social events. To this kook, you're an outsider who just doesn't get it.

Can we all agree that a balanced life is a happy life? Okay, then. Well, these kooks are not in balance; their lives are totally lopsided with all of their attention focused on "the group." Meetings, outreach, potlucks, emergency late-night coffee sessions, three a.m. phone calls, seminars, books on tape, more meetings, workshops...AHHHHH!!! This is WAY beyond recovery. This is a lifestyle. And these kooks are totally convinced that they cannot function without it. What about you? Where do you fit in?

Get With the Program

For the 12-Stepper, everything comes back to "the program," whatever that program may be. It could be AA, NA, or OA. It could be a group focused on recovering from cancer, post-traumatic stress, or crummy childhoods. The "program" could also be for ex-gays, former prostitutes, soldiers released from active duty, or any other group of people dealing with their previous lives, looking for a fresh start.

Again, support groups can be awesome. But the 12-Stepper takes it about ten steps too far. Rather than use it as a tool on the path to recovery, this kook filters everything through the "program." And that includes your life, too. Twelve-Steppers believe that everyone can and should benefit from the wisdom endowed by the "program," expecting you to get on board regardless of your personal experience, beliefs, or values. You may not have to attend meetings or gatherings, but you WILL be expected to respect and adhere to the rules imposed by the "program." Why not? It's only for your benefit, right? You couldn't possibly be happy just the way you are? Could you?

If you're dating a 12-Stepper, there's no room or respect for the way you choose to deal with your own issues. When the two of you have a problem, you'll have to solve it using the techniques your kook learned in the "program." And if you ever deign to diss this exalted group your sweetie belongs to, well, you might as well have kicked his cat or ran over her dog. It won't be pretty.

You Just Don't Get It

Part of the initial attraction of joining a support group is the opportunity to be surrounded by individuals who have had similar experiences. Twelve-Steppers start out just wanting to find someone who can relate, wanting to spend time with other people who have been there and done that. But eventually that sense of belonging fosters exclusivity. Unless you're drinking the dishwater coffee and eating stale, grocery store cookies every Tuesday night right along with them, you're S.O.L.

You couldn't possibly get it. You just don't understand. These people know the real me. We know how to help each other. It's the only place where I don't have to explain myself. Where I can just be me.

Great. So you're totally clueless, unable to empathize with the gal you love most. So your guy can't be himself around you and would never look to you for help or solace. Nice. The 12-Stepper is shutting you out AND making you feel bad about the fact that "you just don't get it." That's a double whammy! Not only are you deprived of intimacy with your one true love, it's your own damn fault because you're not one of the group. How the heck are you supposed to get past that? (Hint: You're not going to get past it.)

Twelve-steppers make you feel isolated because you don't belong to the select group of people recovering from the same issue. You'll also end up feeling worthless, useless, and lonely. Eventually you'll wonder why your sweetie ever asked you out in the first place. But while you're busy blaming yourself, the 12-Stepper is using "the group" to put a wall up between you. These kooks may look healthy, but they're still not in the game. Making you feel left out so that you'll get fed up and leave is just a way for them to stay in the shithole that is their life. Fear of losing the group is stronger than the fear of losing you. Aren't you glad you agreed to that second date?

Maybe When I Get Through the Steps...

Are you waiting for your sweetie to make it through all the steps so you can get on with your lives? Holding off on making a commitment to you until he or she has made it through the "program" could be a wise move in preparation for a healthy marriage, or it could just be a sign that your sweetie is a 12-Stepper. How can you tell the difference? Well, how's your dreamboat doing? Is your guy making progress AND making plans with you? Is your gal optimistic that you'll be free to hitch up in the not-too-distant future? Or is your sweetie lost in the steps (or wisdom, or classes, or workshops, or sessions) with no hope of finishing in the next decade?

Committing to finishing the necessary steps toward recovery before committing fully to you is a noble decision. Using the steps as a way to fend off your requests and *avoid* commitment is a major cop out. I'm all for completing the steps, but what if they're never over? What if there are more levels of understanding to be obtained, more depths of spirituality to explore, more painful memories to address? So many more that it seems the steps are really a never-ending staircase to the sky?

Healing is a lifelong process; it's not a destination. There is no finish line, so what's your sweetie waiting for? Nothing. He doesn't want to be done; she's content with her life as is. This is how 12-Steppers feel safe, working toward a life that may never manifest. They like the struggle, the process of becoming. In fact, they like it more than they like you.

Why Do 12-Steppers Do It?

It's no secret that some people replace one addiction with another and that others recover but still hang on to addictive behavior, making them the same old assholes minus the fun part. But remember, being an addict or recovering from a trauma does not make someone a kook. It's an important distinction to make because if you are in love with someone who is making an grand effort to get healthy, you need to muster up patience and kindness, not judgment.

Some people genuinely need time to focus solely on their recovery, and some groups require members to abstain from romantic relationships for a period of time. If that's the case for your sweetie, he or she shouldn't be dating you at all. But 12-Steppers aren't really following group protocol, are they? Nope. In fact, they are using the guidance and requirements of the group as a crutch, a way to distance themselves from reality. And from you.

Recovery groups and other wellness programs can be insular communities wherein everyone is applauded for their efforts and understood completely. Why would anyone want to step outside of that world? The group is a lifeline, a haven, and the calm in the storm. Within the group your guy or gal may feel like a superstar, a shining example of the effectiveness of the "program." Is it any wonder your sweetie has built a life around these people?

Still, you're not asking for much, really. Just to be held in high regard and maybe spend a little more time with your squeeze. Down the line you may want a four-bedroom split-level and a pimped out minivan, but for now, you just want to feel like your guy or gal wants to be in a relationship with you. That's the problem with these kooks. They really don't want to get too involved because it would mean taking a chance on real life and real experiences. Twelve-steppers use their groups as an excuse to disengage and eventually quit trying. But you wouldn't understand. Remember?

You Had Me At Step One (or Why YOU Do It)

There's something about the people who have been through a crisis and come out the other side. They're tough. Inspiring. Mostly optimistic. You like the fact that your guy conquered something major; it gives you comfort to know he's strong. The fact that your gal is willing to change and solicit the help of experts shows you she's not set in her ways. And frankly, it's sort of a turn-on that your sweetie has a tragic and/or checkered past. She's mysterious; he has a been-there-done-that perspective that you find attractive. If you fell for your sweetie sexy, brooding ways, don't kick yourself too hard. You like what you like.

On the other hand, hooking up with a 12-Stepper could also be all about you. You know how wannabe artists date other artists, how people with a dormant travel bug fall in love with globetrotters? Yup. It's just like that. Have you considered the possibility that you might need a little 12-step action yourself? Are you afraid to face your addiction, your lingering fears, or your troubled history? Because it's not uncommon for us to fall for those who are doing something we want or should be doing, who are living a life we want or should be living. We are mirrors, after all, reflections of one another.

Think about it. Does any part of you want just a little bit of the "program" to rub off on you? Are you secretly hoping your guy or gal will guide you to a healthier life? If you are in need of a support group, counselor, or treatment of some kind, the 12-Stepper may be the best kook for you. In fact, you might be made for each other. Two kooks in love. How sweet. (Hey, don't knock it. When it works, it works.)

How to Spot the 12-Stepper

Twelve-steppers are easy to spot once you get past the first few dates. They spend most of their time and energy focused on the group or the "program," so expect to hear about it a lot, and I do mean *a lot*. Here are a few other ways to spot this kook:

- **Can't Make a Solo Decision**

Try as they may, these kooks just can't make a decision on their own. Before they say, "Yea" or "Nay," they first have to consult their support group, sponsor, mentor or some other expert. Does your guy hem and haw when you ask him something yet take definitive action mere moments after one of his "meetings?" Does your gal make a decision and then change it after speaking with her group?

If your sweetie defers to his support group exclusively, if he or she cannot make a move without them, that's a sure sign you're dating a 12-Stepper. This tell is particularly problematic to live with because you end up feeling as though your life is ruled by a group of virtual strangers. And you know what really sucks? Not pulling any weight with your kook. All of us want to feel as though our opinions matter, that our partners support our decisions. It's pretty basic stuff, isn't it? Well, if you're dating a 12-Stepper, you're not gettin' it. Respect, that is. Geez. Why are you still with this kook?

- **Has No (Other) Friends**

When was the last time you went out with one of your sweetie's non-recovery friends? (That time you had dinner with the old high school buddies – whom you *never* saw again – doesn't count.) Still thinking? No problem. Take all the time you need. I'm not going anywhere.

What? Friend count still at zero? Aside from those ever-present twelve-steppers, that is. Well, you tried. I'm not really surprised you couldn't come up with a varied list of your sweetie's peeps. After all, that would require having the time and the desire for a social life outside of the group. It's to be expected that your guy would make some great friends while going through the toughest time of his life, but when he cuts all of his old pals out of his life, he's bordering on kooky. (Unless, of course, they are all jerks, or druggies, or part of what brought him to his knees in the first place.) And if your gal doesn't seem interested in making any new friends outside of the group, you might as well get her a kook tattoo and call it a day.

- **Puts Group Before You**

Like an M.D. on call, 12-Steppers will drop everything to help another member of the group or attend to the needs of the group as a whole. If your guy routinely cancels plans, cuts out on dates early, and generally schedules his life around the group, there's a good chance you're dating a 12-Stepper. If your gal goes out of her way to comfort and care for other group members, even when you need her the most, you might be involved with a 12-Stepper.

Welcome to your new life, second fiddle. If your sweetie is a 12-Stepper, be prepared to wait in line. Your needs will be sacrificed for the greater good – the good of the group, that is. Routinely. The sad fact is these kooks see their recovery program as the top priority, even over you. So if there's drama with the group or program chores to take care of, you're screwed. Unless you join the group. Hey! That's an idea. The old if-you-can't-beat-'em-join-'em adage. If you do, more power to you. A whole room full of 12-Steppers? Yikes!

What if I'm Not Sure?

Okay, I'll give you this one. It's entirely possible your guy or gal is not a 12-Stepper. Recovery is an all-consuming process, especially in the first year, and it could be you've fallen for your sweetie right at the height of it. So how do you know for sure? Here are a few tips to help you scope out the 12-Stepper:

- **Change the Subject**

Try; just try to talk to your sweetie about something other than recovery. Twelve-Steppers are one-note wonders, content to discuss their process, program, or group for hours on end. So change the subject, why don't you? Introduce a new topic of conversation. Engage in a lively discourse about art, politics, or (gasp) even you. If your guy is a 12-Stepper, he won't last long before returning to his favorite subject. But if your gal takes the hint and goes along with it, you may be able to entertain a slight glimmer of hope that she's just going through a much-needed phase.

- **Go to a Neutral Therapist**

I'm guessing you've got a bit of tension around this issue in your relationship. Why not find a couple's therapist to help you through it? The therapist will be able to help you spot this kook in a nanosecond, AND help you deal. A prerequisite of most recovery programs and self-help groups is a member's belief in the methods employed to help them get well. So look for a neutral party, a therapist who is new to both of you and does not have any affiliation with your sweetie's recovery group. If your guy refuses to go with you, or if your gal won't take the therapist seriously, that's a big, bright red flag. Take notice.

- **Broaden Your Horizons**

Time for you and the squeeze to shake things up a bit. Start filling up that schedule with new and fun couple things to do outside of the group. Expand your social network, go on adventures, and seek out interesting experiences. If you can get your guy or gal to say, "No," to a few support-group related events in order to try something new with you, it's a safe bet that you're not dating a 12-Stepper. But if your sweetie freaks at the thought of canceling anything, it's time you face facts. These kooks don't want to broaden their horizons. You've got to ask yourself, how much fun am I going to have with this group-obsessed person?

Life with the 12-Stepper can be lonely and frustrating, especially when you realize your sweetie will always need the group. They're holding him up, making her feel strong, helping Sweetie get through the day. Where do you fit in? Easy. You don't. Unless you met your guy or gal in the group, you'll always be an outsider, someone who wouldn't understand. Twelve-Steppers don't grow out of it, so don't even think about biding your time until the group loses its magnetism. That would be a waste of your precious time.

Isn't it better that my guy is talking it out in church basements instead of sleeping in shelters? Absolutely. Doesn't it help my gal to have a group of people rooting for her rather than try to deal solo? Yes, it does. But don't kid yourself. Just because the group is good for your sweetie doesn't mean it's good for you or your relationship. Time to disconnect. Call it a day and find someone who has room for you and all that you could share together. But if you do have to break up with a 12-Stepper, don't worry too much. 12-Steppers have a whole posse of kooks backing them up. You're doing yours a favor. He or she needs something new to talk about at group anyway.

The Kook In You

So which kook are you? Did you really think this was all about the parade of crazies you've dated? Nope. There's a kook in you, my friend, and the sooner you identify your own kookiness, the faster you'll find your perfect match. (Well, almost perfect. Again, this ain't the movies. How many times do I have to tell you that?)

Maybe you're not a card-carrying kook, but you may have tendencies that *remind* people of kooks they've known and loved. The good news is self-awareness puts a damper on most annoying behavior, so if you're willing to look at your own idiosyncrasies and insecurities, you'll soon eradicate your most kooky traits.

Ask around. Gather up your courage and swallow your pride. If you promise no retribution, the people who love you best will tell you the truth. Call up old lovers and grill them about your foibles and fumbles. Get the lowdown on the kook in you and then take a look at the kooks you've bumped up against over the years. See any similarities? Any patterns? Any warnings blinking at you in bright red neon?

Kooks are drawn to other kooks, foils for their screwed-up lives. They fit together like perfect puzzle pieces, feeding off of each other until dreams are dashed and hearts are broken. Break the cycle. Stop being a magnet for kooks. Face the kook in you so you can avoid all the rest of them. You can do it. And if you need a little help figuring it all out, take the Kook in You Quiz at SpottingTheKooks.com. Get your friends together and make a night of it. A few questions (and a few drinks) in you'll be laughing your ass off and feeling decidedly better about your kooky self.

The Venue Menu

Ah, the greatest mystery of our time: Where to go to find your one true love...or just anyone who is NOT a certifiable kook. Unfortunately, there are no kook-free bars, chat rooms, or gyms. Heck, you could even run into a few at an ice cream social. But while you can't be sure you won't run into a kook in your search for happily ever after, you can find a plethora of qualified candidates if you base where you look on what you want.

Rather than search for the latest "great place to meet people," think about what you like to do and what you've always wanted to try – you're more likely to meet someone who has similar interests, values, or goals. For example, if you're really into downhill skiing, get a season pass and hang out there all of the time. Chances are you'll meet someone who also loves to ski or who is at least *interested* in skiing.

Or if you just can't picture yourself with someone who does not have the same political leanings that you have, dedicate a good portion of your time to volunteering on a campaign or with a grassroots organization working to make the change you'd like to see in the world. Likewise, if you've got specific requirements in a partner, looking for a date outside of those parameters would not be wise no matter how much you want to "just find someone *not* crazy." Best Foods mayo cannot live in the same house with Miracle Whip sandwich spread. Set yourself up for compatibility right up front and you might just find "the one."

Opposites attract, but it doesn't mean they can live together for the rest of their lives, or even until next Tuesday. Increase your odds for a good match by looking for love in all the *right* places. Here's a venue menu to help get your brainstorm on:

THE CLASSICS

Before we jump off into new territory, I must pay homage to the classic pickup venues. They may seem old and tired, but really they are tried and true. You'll meet tons of single folk using any one of these standard methods if you try even just a little, but they are far from kook-proof. Anytime you're just one of the crowd you're in danger of meeting a totally random kook who sweeps you off your feet. Still, I have to give a shout out to the "usual places." Besides, you're armed and ready to spot all kooks, so you might as well give these traditional hot spots another spin:

Bar Scene

You're done with bars; I get that. But maybe a revised approach could change your mind about finding love on Saturday night. In many respects, bars are excellent places to meet potential lovers and others because there are just so many people to choose from! For me, the best perk of going out to bars was the ability to find men who could hold their own on the dance floor. Dance-ability is one of my minimum requirements, so bars and nightclubs with a good dance scene were particularly useful to me.

If you're over the bar scene, be a little more discriminating with both the establishment and your schedule. Check out bars and clubs that suit your interests and style rather than those famous for hoards of horny singles. Once you've identified several you *might* want to go to again, find out about the schedule of events. It's always more fun to go to a bar on open mike or drag bingo night, and you'll likely meet other people who "don't go out much" but really dig karaoke, or drag, or...bingo.

The Beach

Okay, maybe it's a little too *The Hills* or *Baywatch* or any other tacky, trashy, babe-filled primetime soap opera (gotta love those guilty pleasures), but for my money, the beach is still a primo place to land a date. It's free, people are outside having fun, and most everyone is dressed scantily enough to show you the goods without feeling like you have to pay for it. Choose a great location and set up in the late afternoon when the families start going home and the single folks get ready to party. There's nothin' like sitting around a beach bonfire underneath a whole mess of stars to set the right mood.

Blind Dates and Set Ups

Blind dates can suck big time. Can you think of another time you went out with someone *begrudgingly*? But blind dates can also be fun and fruitful, especially when your pals set you up with someone who actually is "perfect for you." If you're on a mission to hook up and settle down, set your pride aside and ask your posse to make good on all of those matchmaking threats. Just remember to first determine the caliber of your friends' judgment – how good is their picker? If your buds have a wonderful partner of their own, always say, "Yes." And keep it causal – just a quick lunch or a stop for a chai tea latte and see how it goes.

Grocery Stores

Cruisin' the produce section, lookin' for love. We've all done it. Maybe on purpose, maybe out of sheer desperation. Still, many a match has been made before and after checkout. The grocery store is the singles' jackpot because a) everyone needs groceries, b) everything in the store is a conversation starter, and c) you can weed out the marrieds just by looking in their carts. And while the grocery store is still rife with kooks, you can spot a few of them if you pay attention to what they buy and how they interact with other shoppers and store staff. Can you really find your soul mate in the frozen food aisle? Absolutely. There's nothing like bonding over Cherry Garcia to get the sparks a flyin'. Two spoons, anyone?

Place of Worship

Places of worship are excellent venues for singles. Many churches and synagogues host a version of the classic mixer, complete with nametags and chaperones. Other places of worship provide exciting activities for eligible singles similar to outdoor and adventure clubs. Just showing up at services is a great way to meet people. Let the powers that be know you're hoping to make new "friends," and you'll soon be accosted with introductions. And don't hunker down at your same old same old; visit a different place of worship every week to widen your pool of potential matches.

Speed Dating

A new classic like online dating, speed dating is a fun and efficient way to meet a ton of people in a short period of time. There's something to be said for first impressions. Speed dating helps you hone your gut instincts because you don't have time to hem and haw and then think again. If you get a funny feeling after two minutes with someone, don't ignore it because they're cute or loaded or totally into you. Otherwise, you'll end up with yet another kook!

Look for speed dating events in your neighborhood and surrounding areas, and make time for one when you're out of town on business or pleasure. Ask for a great kook dating story during each mini-date. It's a unique question that will break the ice, incite laughter, and show you each person's colors – or at least a few of them.

FOR CLASS-LOVIN' TYPES

A love of learning is a fantastic quality in a partner and certainly keeps things interesting when you're feeling bored and oh so "married." In fact, learning new things together is a proven way to foster intimacy and reignite excitement in a relationship. When you meet your one and only in a class about something you enjoy, you have the benefit of shared interests and a mutual willingness to keep things fresh through education.

Adult Education/Continuing Education

Most colleges offer continuing education classes in the evening and on weekends when you are more likely to find people your own age. Other adult education organizations offer classes with a shorter duration, or one-time events, but you'll have to be on your toes to nab a date during 15-minute pee breaks. Remember, if you want to avoid the kooks, you must be totally committed to authenticity. So don't take a class unless you're genuinely into it.

Dance Class

Anyone who is willing to step outside of his or her comfort zone to learn something new is worth checking out. Anyone willing to look silly in front of a mirrored wall is worthy of a second look. And anyone who is willing to do all that in a room full of strangers is, well, totally awesome.

Dance class, be it tap, ballroom, or hip hop is a great way to meet people who want to take a bite out of life. Look for a dance class specifically for singles so you don't end up in a room full of couples. Or choose a class that does not involve partner dancing. Sign up for evening classes; otherwise you may end up hanging out with the soccer moms and senior citizens. That is, unless that's what you're in to. Whatever floats your boat!

Self-Improvement Workshops

So you're getting your life together, learning how to do this or that better and faster. You're committed to your own self-improvement. You're gaining a deeper knowledge of your body, mind and soul. Here's the thing: If you're going to find a compatible mate, you're going to have to find someone who also drank the Kool-Aid. If your partner is not on the same path toward enlightenment, it's never going to work out.

Find a way to connect with other people who are on a similar journey toward a better whatever. Attend classes, workshops, and other events related to your preferred method of self-improvement. Get involved with the event by volunteering to sit at the registration table, take notes, or sell raffle tickets – whatever you can do that will get you a face-to-face with as many people as possible. And if there are no social or educational events related to this path you've chosen, find one online and join the community.

Other Class Ideas: Pilates, spinning, yoga and other exercise classes; martial arts and self-defense classes; baking, brewing, and cooking classes; classes related to your favorite hobbies, such as photography or sailing; religious or spiritual instruction; foreign language classes.

FOR JOINER TYPES

Are you passionate about art? Mad for water skiing? Obsessed with motorcycles, knitting, or making cheese? Somewhere there's a club for whatever you're super psyched about, a group of people who share your fascination with Victorian literature, the Civil War, or independent film. Clubs are an excellent venue for dating, and many of them are singles-only for that very reason. Find a club that is well organized with lots of members and go for it. The worst thing that could happen is you'll make a few friends while you enjoyed your favorite hobby.

Book Clubs

Discussing stories and ideas with the one you love is pretty romantic. You'll find all sorts of sexy bookish types when you join a book club, people who care about art or history or the state of the world. What could be better than falling for someone who loves mystery novels just as much as you do? And all of those nonfiction exposes you've got lined up on that sagging bookshelf? You just might find someone who actually thinks that's cool. PLUS, you'll be sure to find someone who actually (gasp!) *can read.*

Book clubs come in every size, from a small group of friends who get together every week to dish about characters and nosh to a large gathering of virtual strangers who meet once a month to discuss the same book and get their drink on. Beyond the living room, book clubs are hosted in obvious places such as libraries and bookstores and in coffee shops and places of worship. Some clubs are serious, some are just for fun, but all of them are a great place to meet the love of your life.

Kennel Clubs

Going to the park with your dog in the hopes of getting a date for Friday night is the oldest trick in the book (well, maybe not the *oldest*). If you try this method, you might as well hold up a sign that says, "Over Here, Kooks!" Sure that total stranger is cute and cuddly looking, just like your dog, but you've got nothing else to go on.

Not true with kennel clubs. You've got to really love dogs to join one because very soon club activities become a central part of your life. But when you meet people through kennel club events you know they probably love dogs (almost) as much as you do. And if you're not into dogs, find a horseback riding club or a group for cat lovers. Animals are better judges of character than most humans, so you're off to a good start. Your animals may even be able to spot the kook before you do!

Outdoor Clubs

Picture it: You're canoeing down a lazy river with a hottie as your co-pilot when your group spots a perfect spot for a picnic of fruit, cheese and bread and local wine poured from stainless steel thermoses. Sounds lovely and romantic and healthy to me – and I'm not even the outdoor type! (Hint: Never fake the outdoor thing or you'll end up camping the national parks for the rest of your life.) Take note of those people with really new gear – are they for real or just hunting for nature-lovers? Do they look like experienced skiers or lodge bunnies? You're joining the club to hang out with other outdoor freaks (pardon me, I couldn't help myself), and you want to be sure they're on the up and up.

Outdoor clubs are so common you can find one for almost any proclivity, gender, and age group. Some are focused solely on one type of activity while others mix it up with a variety of outdoor experiences. Getting sweaty with strangers is a much more effective way to break the ice than say, making small talk at a stiff cocktail party. Besides, you're less likely to find some of the kooks described in this book hoofing it on a trail or wiping out on the bunny slope.

Other clubs: Adventure, travel, and workout clubs; art, film, and music clubs; gardening, neighborhood associations, and other civic clubs; boating, fishing, sailing, and swimming clubs; wine and brew clubs and other project-oriented groups; bargain hunters and other shopping clubs; quilting, scrapbooking, sewing and other craft clubs.

FOR DO-GOODER TYPES

A generous spirit is a must-have quality in a long-term partner, which is why charities are perfect venues to find date-worthy men and women. If you have time to donate, volunteering for a cause that is near and dear to your heart is a great way to meet other like-minded people. Besides, volunteering puts everyone in a good mood, so if you do find someone you'd like to go out with, you'll be off to a good start. Nonprofits are very co-ed and usually draw a unique mix of people – yet another reason to volunteer. Just don't get stuck in the office answering phones or preparing mailings. Be specific about the type of work you'd like to do, a job that gets you out in the world, meeting as many people as possible.

Animal Rescue/Animal Adoption

If you have a genuine love of all things furry (don't go there), sign up to help out with your local animal rescue or animal shelter. In general, animal lovers are kind to humans too, and as I mentioned earlier, animals are terrific judges of character. Best of all, adorable pets are people magnets. Volunteer to help walk cooped up dogs or participate in awareness events where you're sure to meet bunches of four-legged fanatics.

But the single best volunteer job for singles on the hunt is the animal adoption table, you know, the one stationed outside the grocery store, the one you can never pass by without stopping to nuzzle a homeless cutie-pie? Offer to help man the table and you'll meet more people than you can count, let alone date.

Fundraising

Rub elbows with the movers and shakers on fundraising committees, areas of nonprofits that are always open to new members. Most are full of passionate people looking to make a real difference as well as network with other volunteers. A BIG bonus to volunteers is access to some of the best parties and events in town, which are totally fun to help organize.

Or if you don't have time to volunteer, become a donor to your favorite charity or arts organization. "Major donor" status can be achieved for less than you think, granting you access to the exclusive events. Patrons of theaters and other arts organization get exciting perks, such as meeting talent, sitting in on rehearsals, and getting a first look at openings. AND you'll meet other people who are committed to the work of the nonprofit you've chosen to support, so you're already bonded over something pretty darn cool.

Volunteer Vacations

You've got to admire someone who "gives up" two precious weeks to help African villages get access to clean water or to help clean up debris in hurricane-ravaged New Orleans. Volunteer vacations are all the rage and offer opportunities to make a difference in almost every country in the world. If you're passionate about helping those in need and want to meet other people with the same values, sign up to volunteer during your next break. You'll see the world, make a significant difference in people's lives, and get to know your fellow volunteers really, really well. And if you do find Mr. or Mrs. Right in a Costa Rican jungle, you'll be bonded for life.

Other Do-Gooder Venues: Man outreach tables and gift-wrapping tables for your favorite charity; sign up with Habitat for Humanity or another project-oriented charity; go local and volunteer at soup kitchens, homeless shelters, low-income day care centers, nursing homes, or hospitals; start your own program to give back and recruit friends, colleagues, and their friends and colleagues to help out.

Other Venue Ideas

When you choose a venue based on genuine interest, almost any venue is a great place to meet your next date. The closer you hone in on your own values and aspirations, the more apt you are to find "the one," or at least avoid some kooks. Here are a few more venue ideas you may want to try:

- Shopping venues such as local farmers markets, furniture stores, craft fairs, trade shows and gift shows, garage sales, flea markets, antique malls, shopping parties, and super sale events.
- Art and cultural venues such as museum and gallery openings, fringe festivals and other theater festivals, film festivals, art walks and art crawls, music in the park, auctions, and author readings.
- Sports venues such as walks, runs, and bike-a-thons for charity, the gym, league sports, tournaments, minor league games, informal meet-ups such as Ultimate Frisbee or Volleyball, and Tai chi in the park.
- Food-related venues such as wine tastings, cooking parties, food and wine shows, state fairs, bake sales, and restaurant openings.

Online Dating

I know, I know, there's a stigma attached to online dating. Look, you aren't the first person to meet someone online, and you won't be the last. Some of the dating websites have seriously sophisticated programs that could help you find someone who meets all of your criteria and then some. That's a lot of work to do solo and a lot of nights out when you could be perusing eligible bachelors and bachelorettes in your PJs and slippers. Besides, what if your one true, non-kook love is 5,000 miles and two time zones away? How else are you going to meet?

If you're not sure which dating site to sign up with, or need help figuring it all out, I've reviewed most of the sites here: http://loly.co, which is an online dating site I created that you really should know.

Certified Kook Spotter

You sure can spot 'em. Kooks don't stand a chance with you. You've honed your scoping skills and can spot a kook in disguise hiding behind bushes three miles away. You can't be fooled, and you won't be coerced into dating anyone who doesn't seem on the up and up. You're strong, aware of your own kooky past and how that makes you vulnerable to other kooks. You're living a life of authenticity, not pretending to be someone else in the hopes of landing a dream come true. And you'll wait. You'll wait for the right guy or gal to show up and fit right into that master plan of yours, maybe even shake it up a bit, make it even better than you imagined.

YOU are a certified kook spotter. Congrats! Life will be so much better now, so much more fun and free and full of hope. 'Cause somewhere out there is another non-kook looking for someone just like you. And when you meet that exceptional person and finally feel good about saying, "Yes," send me pictures, okay? I want details.

    Onward...

About the Authors

Adryenn Ashley

Unabashed author Adryenn Ashley's sassy award winning style combined with her expansive knowledge of sex and practical steps to protecting yourself and your hard earned assets, make wise readers of her book series on relationship advice for women. Bringing humor and attitude to an otherwise touchy, challenging subject, Ashley makes the information totally digestible and relatable. Ashley's qualifications as a sex tech entrepreneur and relationship advocate bring rock-solid credibility to the valuable advice in her writings. Her Sex and the City meets Dr. Ruth approach is sure to make the savvy, modern, single girls loyal followers.

Anjanette Harper

AJ Harper is an award-winning editor and publishing strategist. She has helped hundreds of authors—from newbies to New York Times bestselling authors with millions of books sold—develop significant and loyal followings, grow their brand and secure lucrative deals for follow-up books.

As a developmental editor, AJ's clients' books have won many national awards and have been chosen for numerous "best of" lists. For 2016, her authors' books received 14 prestigious award nominations and five awards, and two novels were chosen for "Best of 2016" lists in Publishers Weekly and Kirkus Reviews (one of only six books in their respective genres).

www.ingramcontent.com/pod-product-compliance
Lightning Source LLC
LaVergne TN
LVHW052257070426
835507LV00036B/3097